The Wired World

An introduction to the theory and practice of the information society

The Wired World

An introduction to the theory and practice of the information society

James Dearnley and John Feather
Department of Information Science,
Loughborough University

LIBRARY ASSOCIATION PUBLISHING
LONDON

© James Dearnley and John Feather 2001

Published by
Library Association Publishing
7 Ridgmount Street
London WC1E 7AE

www.la-hq.org.uk/lapublishing

Library Association Publishing is wholly owned by The Library Association.

First published 2001

British Library Cataloguing in Publication Data

A catalogue record for this book is available from the British Library.

ISBN 1-85604-373-8

Typeset from authors' disk in 11/14pt New Baskerville and Swiss 721 by Library Association Publishing.
Printed and made in Great Britain by MPG Books Ltd, Bodmin, Cornwall.

Contents

Preface

The information society is everywhere. Or is it? The phrase is used by politicians, academics and journalists with a multitude of meanings, and sometimes with none. It is probably associated in many people's minds with the world wide web, with e-commerce, with distance learning, with electronic games and with dozens of other manifestations of computing. There can certainly be no doubt of the power and impact of the computer. It has changed almost everything we do. It is argued, however, that the computer has been more than merely an instrument of change – it has actually been the cause of a change so profound that the society in which we now live needs a new name. Great works of scholarship have been devoted to this proposition, and profound thinkers have addressed the issues which it raises.

Our aim in this book is modest. We are addressing those who are probably confronting these issues systematically for the first time. Many of our readers will, no doubt, be students who are preparing for a career in some aspect of information provision or information management. We have three basic aims:

- to explore the underlying theories of the information society as they have been developed by sociologists, scientists and economists
- to consider the concept of information and how it is stored and communicated through various media and technologies
- to examine some of the ways in which an information society is being developed and what shape that development might take in the future.

This takes us into a large number of issues, and we make no apologies for the breadth of our approach. We range from information theory, communication theory and information science through broadcasting and publishing to the political dimension of the information society. We draw on the work of sociologists, economists, political analysts and historians, as well as that of information scientists and information theorists. We have tried to consider the growth of the *idea* of an information society as well as its actual manifestations. That draws us into such issues as the development of an economy based on the delivery of services and knowledge creation. We consider the issues of public policy and private behaviour which arise out of this. And we have chosen to look in some depth at the European Union – the world's largest single economy – to see how some of these issues are being addressed at a level at which they have an impact on millions of people.

Because this book is intended to be introductory to most of the topics on which it touches, we have added some suggestions for further reading. These take two forms: at the end of each chapter, we have highlighted a few of the publications and websites cited in that chapter which we feel will be particularly helpful, and at the end of the book, we have made some more general suggestions. Finally, in addition to a conventional bibliography that lists all the works cited (in all formats and media), we have given a select list of relevant websites with a commentary on them.

We hope that our readers will gain some insight from us into the society in which they will work, and which, as information professionals, they will help to mould.

James Dearnley
John Feather

1

Theorizing the information society

Introduction

'Information' is one of the buzzwords of our times. We are told that we live in an *information age*, that we suffer from *information overload*, that ours is an *information society*, that we are dependent on *information technology*. There is an academic discipline of *information science*, there is a subject called *information theory*, there are professional people called *information managers*. And there is both confusion and imprecision about what some of this actually means. The dictionary definition of 'information' is 'something told, knowledge' according to one source,[1] 'knowledge acquired through experience or study' according to another.[2] To confuse matters even further 'knowledge' is an almost equally elusive word. It is 'awareness or familiarity gained by experience . . . a person's range of information',[3] or 'the facts, feelings or experiences known by a person . . . specific information about a subject'.[4] Clearly the relationship between knowledge and information is both close and complicated. In this first chapter, we seek to disentangle some of the confusion through a consideration of some of the thinking which underlies our understanding of our information-conscious world.

Thinking about the nature of knowledge and information and their impact on society is not new, even if some of the language would have been unfamiliar to earlier generations. It has long been recognized that information is the key to power, and that education is the key to the acquisition of information. In early medieval England, for example, there was a gradual increase in the reliance on written documents as evidence of the legal rights and duties of individuals and institutions.[5] Inevitably, this put a greater emphasis on the value and necessity of literacy, and gave the literate power over the illiterate. As literacy increased, the prestige of orality decreased and there was even greater pressure to learn to read.[6] The invention of printing in the middle of the 15th century made reading matter more widely available, and gave further impetus to existing trends towards the development of a literate society dependent upon written rather than purely spoken language as the gateway to knowledge, information and power.[7]

These juxtapositions were at least implicit in the concerns of the 17th-century English philosopher, John Locke. Two of his most important works were concerned, respectively, with education and with political power. Locke had a clear view of the objective of education. To him, it was 'every Man's indispensible duty to do all the Service he can to his Country'. It was because 'this subject is of so great concernment, and a right way of Education is of so general Advantage', that he felt obliged to write about it.[8] Locke was an early advocate of helping children to learn by making learning enjoyable, by reading such books as Aesop's *Fables* as well as the Bible and the Catechism. He was regarded by later generations as one of the progenitors of the idea of liberal, child-centred education. He was also an early advocate of a more open society; in his *Two treatises of government* he developed the idea of the social contract between the ruler and the ruled, in which the sovereign power of the people was ceded to the ruler in return for protection and good government, but could, if the ruler failed, be retrieved by the sovereign people and handed to others.[9] Locke's ideas were used to justify the English Revolution of 1688[10] and, both directly and as they were embodied in the writings of later authors in Britain, France and America, they were to be influential in the American and French Revolutions in 1774 and 1789 respectively. It is no accident that the liberal educational theorist and the liberal political philosopher were one and the same person. Locke's educated people were capable of understanding his civil society and its social contract, and they alone were qualified to exercise their rights in it.

A long history thus underlies the current assumption of a symbiotic relationship between literacy, education and an open society, and is central to an understanding of the so-called information society of the early 21st century. As we shall see, the political agenda for the development of the information society is essentially driven by an assumption that such development is desirable because it both facilitates and embeds democratic institutions and principles. Participation in the information society is regarded as essential to participation in society at large, and in some countries is becoming indispensable. This must be understood, however, in an even broader context.

The *information society* is only one of several phrases which we use to describe the contemporary world. Two of particular importance to us are significant in their wording, for both reflect an attempt to recognize the difference between our society and its immediate predecessor.

The concept of *post-modernism* at first seems like a contradiction in terms, and if 'modern' is equated with 'contemporary' then indeed it is. But as a cultural descriptor, 'post-modernism' is a statement about a culture that has grown out of and away from the self-proclaimed 'modernism' of the mid-20th century, the world of Picasso, James Joyce and Frank Lloyd Wright. Post-modernism takes many forms, and the word is not always used in the same sense by different writers. In broad terms, it is best understood as an approach to the analysis of society and culture that does not seek general explanations or absolute standards. At one level, this might mean, for example, that Blur can be argued to be 'as good as' Beethoven, although many post-modern theorists would reject the whole notion of such comparisons and indeed of absolutist terms such as 'good' or 'bad'. In a different context, the post-modern view of society is that it is fragmented and multifaceted. No single doctrine (such as Marxism or Christianity) or structural economic theory (such as monetarism) can be taken as a general explanation. Everything must be individually analysed and explained in its own terms.[11]

The second phrase that contrasts us with the past is the *post-industrial society*, which again seems like a contradiction and indeed to be factually inaccurate. We manifestly live in a world of industries that extract and process raw materials, manufacture goods and provide services. The phrase, however, refers to a very specific form of industrial organization, sometimes called Fordism,[12] in which the economies of advanced counties were dominated by mass-production industries based on production line techniques. The implication is that the economy is now driven by the provision of services, not by the production of goods. The phrase was used as early as 1917 by Arthur J. Perry, an American Guild Socialist, in his *Old worlds for new: a study of the post-industrial state*, and intermittently thereafter, but it became common only after World War 2.[13] By the fourth quarter of the 20th century, it seemed that western societies were beginning to define themselves by what they were not, recognizing that they were different but not yet fully able to define the difference. The sense of coming to the end of an era was pervasive. One distinguished historian became an international guru by proclaiming the 'end of history',[14] and there were plenty prepared to follow in his wake.

The adoption of the concept of the information society can be seen in part as an attempt to produce a more positive definition of difference. But we should not confuse difference with novelty. Locke's argument that education benefits society as a whole as well as individuals, and that is it therefore a civic duty both to provide it and to acquire it, reminds us that knowledge and information have long been understood by some to be a public good. Why, then, do we see such a fundamental difference between ourselves and earlier eras? Are we wrong? Or has there been profound change?

Part of the answer to these questions lies in an understanding of technological change, but only a part. We shall understand more of what has happened and what is happening if we consider some of those who have contributed to our thinking on these matters and have created the intellectual climate in which we are living and working. Essentially there are three strands in the story, which must, in due course, be woven together. In chronological order, these are:

* a growing recognition of the need to provide systematic information to sustain other activities, especially scientific research; it was this that led to the development of what we now call *information science*
* a desire to understand the nature of information itself, and the development of *information theory*
* attempts to develop general social theories that bring together

such concepts as knowledge, information and communication, which have led to the development of theories of the *information society*.

Understanding information

Information science

The phrase 'information science' did not come into regular use until the 1950s,[15] but much of what it embodies has a much earlier origin, which is perhaps best marked by the foundation of the Fédération Internationale de Documentation in Brussels in 1895.[16] The concept of *documentation*, which FID was founded to promote, was essentially about the provision of information to scientists, especially those working in industry, by developing more effective methods for abstracting, information retrieval and the delivery of information to end users. In the 1920s, an English librarian, Samuel Bradford, began to formulate a theory that was to underpin much of the subsequent development of information science. Bradford actually saw himself as a documentalist (in the continental sense) rather than a librarian, and was indeed active in FID of which he was President in 1945. He spent his entire career at what was then the Science Library at South Kensington,[17] and studied how scientific literature was used. He concluded that the useful literature of any discipline (as defined by subsequent citation) was a small and mathematically predictable sub-set of the whole, but that its location (as opposed to its extent) was less predictable and thus required comprehensive indexing and abstracting services to achieve maximum beneficial effect through widespread dissemination and use. Bradford's Law of Scatter, in which these observations and conclusions are embodied, is one of the cornerstones of information science both in theory and in practice.[18]

Bradford was a practitioner who sought to understand more about what he was doing and how he could best serve his clients. His interest in theory derived from this practical consideration rather than *vice versa*, and indeed the essential empiricism of information science, as it is typically understood and practised in the English-speaking world, has remained one of its distinguishing characteristics. Bradford's work had arisen out of the same practical problems that had led to the foundation of FID – the exponential growth of scientific literature, made more complex by the fact that until the second half of the 20th century this literature was in three languages (English, German and French) rather than in the one (English) that came eventually to predominate.[19] By the middle of the century, the phenomenal growth of the literature was presenting a serious problem to scientists, to the extent that in 1948 the Royal Society mounted a major conference, which is seen as a landmark in the development of the discipline.[20] The inspiration was the physicist J. D. Bernal, who had addressed some of the fundamental issues of scientific publication, communication and information in a seminal work published in 1939.[21] The Royal Society conference, and the publication of Bradford's *Documentation* in the same year, led to a wider interest in the whole subject and to attempts to develop more formal theories to explain what was happening.

As the growth of scientific literature continued unabated, scientists and librarians alike were confronted with a problem of ever-increasing complexity. Among some scientists there was almost a sense of the loss of control of their own disciplines;[22] these scientists and the librarians looked to new technologies rather than merely to new techniques to enable them to redress the balance. The possibilities of using mechanical and electronic machines as tools for information science was not ignored at the 1948 conference,[23] but it was not until the late 1950s that it was becoming possible to conceptualize how this might work, and then to translate concept into practice.[24]

By the mid-1960s, information science, as an empirical discipline that underpinned the delivery of information services, was well established. The theoretical basis of the subject was a claim to analyse and describe the characteristics of information and the nature of the information transfer process; but this was achieved by a study of how information was assembled, collected, disseminated and used, rather than by a strictly theoretical approach. This was the basis of the definition offered by Hal Borko in the USA in 1968:

[Information science] is an interdisciplinary science that investigates the properties and behaviour of information, the forces that govern the flow of information, and the techniques, both manual and mechanical, of processing information for optimal storage, retrieval and dissemination.[25]

This was described as 'typical' and '[a definition] which would received widespread assent' in 1987.[26] A decade later, the British scholar R. T. Bottle offered a definition that was essentially similar:

> [Information science is] a discipline which investigates the characteristics of information and the nature of the information transfer process, whilst not losing sight of the practical aspects of collecting, collating and evaluating information and organising its dissemination through appropriate intellectual apparatus and technology.[27]

It would seem that there is a general consensus about the nature of the discipline, and notably so about the importance of its practical applications.

Information theory

The empirical work of the early information scientists – as they came to be known – was essentially intended to help in the management of library collections (especially collections of scientific periodicals) and in the provision of information to research scientists in industry and in the academic world. Despite the name that was used to describe the discipline, there were those who denied that it was, in a traditional sense, a science at all. The German scholar, Gernot Wersig, has provided what is perhaps the best articulated expression of this reservation. To Wersig, information science is a 'post-modern' rather than a 'classical' science, precisely because the problems that it seeks to solve are essentially practical rather than theoretical.[28] Even Bottle, in quoting Wersig with perhaps a hint of disagreement or even disapproval, concedes that 'we are still awaiting our Linnaeus, our Mendeleyev, or even our Keynes'.[29]

What is now called information theory is partly a development of information science, but its most important aspects emerged independently of it. In the very year in which Bernal and his fellow scientists in London were pondering the problems of coping with the seemingly unending growth of scientific literature, the American mathematician Claude E. Shannon was contemplating what he saw as a very different problem. He too was an applied scientist, working on telecommunications at the Bell Laboratories in New Jersey. In order to understand better how to optimize the communication of signals between source and destination, he developed a mathematically based theory of communication.[30] Shannon used probability theory to derive a method for determining the optimal number of binary-coded signs that were needed to send any given signal. From this, he derived a further theory in which he showed how to relate the frequency of any given sign to the probability that it contained relevant information. It was this latter strand of his work that was developed by Shannon himself and by Warren Weaver; this was published in 1949.[31] The Shannon and Weaver model has the essential characteristic of a true scientific theory – universal applicability. It has proved invaluable in understanding the process by which information is transmitted. In essence, they argued that for the message to be effectively transmitted, the originator and the receiver must have a common language (which might be pictorial or mathematical rather than textual) and comparable skills (an appropriate level of literacy or numeracy, for example) and, where relevant, compatible technologies (telephones in the original formulation, but more recently computers).

Shannon also identified and described the phenomenon which he called 'redundancy'. The essence of the redundancy principle is that in any message there are redundant elements, and the message will not lose its force if the redundant elements are truncated or omitted. This is most easily understood in terms of spoken language. Thus, in speech we might say 'see you' meaning 'I will see you again soon', or 'I will see you tomorrow' or 'this evening' or whenever it might be. It might also be totally non-specific, and mean 'I will see you some time'. It might even mean 'I suppose I shall have to see you again even though I do not want to'! The context, understood by both parties and therefore unnecessary to express, actually gives full meaning to 'see you'. The omissions which allow us to say 'see you' and be understood are, in Shannon's terminology, redundancies. The important consequence of the redundancy principle is that a message can be reduced to essential elements without losing its meaning. It also allows for some parts of the message to be lost without necessarily invalidating the message or rendering it meaningless. The redundancy phenomenon does not only allow for imperfections in the electrical or electronic communication of data; it also allows compression of data to achieve maximum cost-effectiveness in transmission. For telephony and telegraphy this was important; for computers it was to prove critical.

The Shannon and Weaver model is now seen as the starting point and an essential foundation of information theory because it is an attempt to measure the quantity and quality of information. It has also proved attractive to information scientists, for it offers a conceptual explanation of the process of the communication of information, which is the subject of their empirical study.[32] It has been argued that information scientists have accepted, too easily, a rather simplified version of Shannon's ideas, but it is typical of the discipline that they have done so – if at all – because this is the most practical way in which to apply them.[33] Subsequent scholars developed the theory in different ways, especially in relation to the development of cognitive science in the 1970s. This was in turn closely linked to the urgent need to conceptualize new generations of computers and the application of the science of cybernetics. The cognitive scientists argued that information arises out of a specific process and set of circumstances, but is itself objective. If this is accepted, then it follows that the process of cognition can be replicated in computers; cognitive science thus underpins the development of computer programs that seek to analyse and process information. The cognitive approach to information theory was widely accepted in the 1970s and 1980s, and is still recognized as being valuable and valid.[34]

Cybernetics, the science of automatic control systems, was another by-product of mathematical theories applied to practical problems. Its founder, the American mathematician Norbert Wiener, was investigating the trajectories of artillery shells when he evolved a statistically based theory about control systems and communications engineering.[35] Cybernetics (his term) concerns itself with the control of communications systems, and again is of particular importance in computing. In the field of information theory, cybernetics and systems science offer an approach that has, somewhat ironically, brought information theory close to the realm of social science. In particular, there is important interaction between the work of information theorists and the thinking of the social theorist Jürgen Habermas, whose ideas have had a significant influence on the development of the concept of the information society.[36]

The development of information theory has been long and uncertain, and has come from many directions. The purely scientific, indeed mathematical, approach that characterized the work of Shannon, Weaver and Wiener, has been supplemented by the work of information scientists with their more empirical traditions. There is consequently no generally accepted theory of information, although there is a broad acceptance that information theory as a field is concerned with the reduction of complexity in the communication of information. But Wersig's comments on information science are almost equally applicable to information theory;[37] it has developed out of the perceived need to resolve practical problems in the communication of information, rather than in the desire to explain observations or a data-set.

The problem lies in the nature of information itself. In one sense it is a phenomenon ('information-as-thing' in the words of Michael Buckland[38]), but it is also a construct (Buckland's 'information-as-knowledge') and the basis of an action ('information-as-process'). It has even been argued that information has a physical existence, with an entropy that can be the subject of mathematical equations.[39] Certainly there is a case to be made that information is not confined to documents, but also exists in natural objects and non-documentary human artefacts.[40] Any museum, with its collections of objects ranging from furniture to fossils, exemplifies this, for all yield information about the past.

The paradox with which we began this chapter returns to haunt us: there is a relationship between information and knowledge, but we have not yet formulated a generally accepted understanding of what it is. The closest we have come is that information is the basis of knowledge and that knowledge is the physical manifestation of information.

Information theory, and the conceptualization of information itself, is of more than purely academic interest, for without a broadly understood common theoretical framework information science has a shaky conceptual base despite its empirical successes and soundness. In turn, that has implications for our understanding of the information society. Indeed, a further paradox is that our conceptualization and understanding of the information society has largely come from disciplines other than information science, and particularly from sociology. One of the issues to which we shall return is the implication of this for information science itself (and indeed for information scientists), for there is a danger of it (and them) being marginalized in the very society with which it and they share a name.

The information society

The essential characteristic of an information society is argued to be that information is its most powerful economic and social agent. It is therefore dominated by occupations that are information dependent, and the technologies that support information storage, processing and dissemination are in common use.[41] It has become common to regard the American social scientist, Daniel Bell, as the first theorist of the information society, and the proponent of its principal characteristics. This view has not gone unchallenged and, while it is indeed true that Bell plays a crucial part in the story, he is not the only player; his role is sometimes confusing to those whose own intellectual background is in information science and information theory.[42] As we have implied, the dependence on information for some activities is far older than our contemporary obsession with it. Nevertheless, there has been real change, and attempts to define the information society reflect the fact that those changes are still incomplete and have been subject to many influences from many different directions.

Machlup's analysis

It was in economic terms that the changes were first identified and their consequences predicted. Fritz Machlup, an economist trained in Vienna before spending the bulk of his distinguished academic career in the USA, was the first to attempt a detailed analysis of the changes that were taking place in the 1950s and early 1960s.[43] His first great work on the subject, published in 1962, is regarded as a landmark in the study of the economic changes that were creating an information society.[44] The essence of Machlup's argument was that the production of knowledge had an economic significance comparable to the production of goods. In post-war America, the greatest industrial power in the history of the world, this was a startling thesis. America's economic dominance was partly a consequence of the fact that she was not only on the winning side in World War 2 but that she was, uniquely among the major allied powers, undamaged by the war itself. Such an advantage could only be temporary, so that relative industrial and economic decline could be argued to have been inevitable.[45] But in the 1940s and 1950s the war itself, and the subsequent Cold War between the USA and the Soviet Union, was a positive boost to those parts of US heavy industry concerned with production of weapons and military equipment.[46] However, the USA's distinctive contribution to industrial output – mass production – was rapidly imitated by her competitors, and indeed by her former enemy, Japan, more effectively than by any of her wartime allies. The Fordist model was adapted by the Japanese to create their own motor-car industry, for example, which, by the time that Machlup was analysing the American economy, was beginning to challenge American hegemony.[47]

Machlup was essentially an economic analyst, not a social prophet. His book is dominated by the statistical data revealed by his research. The novelty lay in the subject of his research and the nature of his data. Rather than looking at the output of goods, Machlup examined expenditure on such matters as education, research and development, broadcasting and legal services. The 'industries' with which he was concerned were not the producers of motor cars, chemicals or steel, but the producers of books, newspapers, television and radio programmes, gramophone records and motion pictures. Machlup's argument was that all these forms of production were knowledge-related; they were either dependent upon knowledge (education), or were a form of knowledge dissemination (publishing) or, crucially, were concerned with production of new knowledge (research and development). His most significant findings lay in his analysis of the relationship between these forms of production and the labour force, summarized in Table 1.1.

Table 1.1   *The knowledge workforce in the USA in 1900 and 1959* [48]

	1900	1959
Knowledge activities	10.7%	31.6%
Non-knowledge activities	89.3%	68.4%

The growth in the proportion of the labour force in knowledge-related occupations between 1900 and 1959 was a result of steady decade by decade increases, an economic and social revolution which had happened silently in the very years when Fordism was at its height. Machlup also had data that suggested future trends. He correlated the size of the knowledge-occupation workforce with the number of full-time students in Grade 9 or higher, that is those likely to progress to what would, in British terms, be called further or higher education. He took the size of the knowledge workforce and the number of students in that category as the total *potential* knowledge workforce; decade by decade, this was an reasonable predictor of the growth of the knowledge occupations, and between 1949 and 1959 it had grown from 37.9% of the total potential workforce to 42.8%.[49]

Machlup's work exposed for the first time the extent to which a modern state, even one that was industrially powerful, was dependent on its knowledge workforce. This became a matter of concern to the US government, which commissioned and published a major analysis of the information economy by Marc Uri Porat.[50] Porat attempted a fundamental redefinition of the structure of the economy, adding a new category – the information sector – to the traditional agricultural, industrial and service sectors. He subdivided this into primary (where the principal product was information) and secondary (where the product or service was information-oriented). Most startlingly, perhaps, he then described the rest of the economy (the three traditional sectors) as the non-information workforce. Implicit in Porat's classification was a bold, but increasingly valid, claim: that the United States' economy was coming to be dependent upon, and dominated by, what Machlup had called the production and distribution of knowledge. Porat's own estimate was that about 50% of the American workforce was now in the information sector. His classification of the workforce has not gone unchallenged,[51] but further refinements of Porat's methods by subsequent analysts still showed well in excess of 40% of the total economically active population engaged in information functions in the early 1990s.[52]

The work of Machlup and Porat was designed to provide a statistical framework for understanding an information-based, or knowledge-driven, economy. Neither of them was concerned with making fine distinctions between knowledge and information, and indeed

Machlup dealt with the question rather dismissively, despite the fact that his citations suggest that he was acquainted with at least some of the growing literature of information theory.[53] The economic phenomena that Machlup described and which Porat transformed into economic predictions had massive social implications, which were not lost on others, even if they were of little interest to the economists. It is in this context that the work of Daniel Bell is most relevant. Bell was a social theorist. In what is perhaps his most famous work, he attempted, in his own words, 'a social forecast about a change in the social framework of Western society'.[54] He called this change 'post-industrial', a concept which had been in his own thinking for several years before his book was written and published.[55]

Bell's social forecast

Machlup's work provided Bell with a factual infrastructure for his observations of the social consequences of economic change in the USA. The essence of his thesis is that there was a change from the production of goods to the provision of services, and that this was underpinned by the production of knowledge. As he developed the fullest version of this thesis in the early 1970s, it was already possible to predict that computers and information technology would play a key role in future developments, although at this stage Bell saw them (not entirely without reason) as primarily tools for the mathematicians who would theorize and quantify the predictive process. In a long section that deals with the importance of technological change in the creation of the post-industrial society, Bell says little about the potential of computers, concentrating instead on more traditional technologies such as those of transport and power sources.[56] He did, however, see knowledge production as the key to technological change and its application in the economy, and for this reason he found Machlup's work particularly attractive. It can be argued that Bell misunderstood what Machlup had shown, or that he did not fully analyse its implications,[57] but in a sense that does not matter. What does matter is the consequence, for it has led to a number of confusions in subsequent thinking, which we need to try to disentangle.

Machlup's dismissal of the need to distinguish between knowledge and information was not inappropriate in his own work. The knowledge industry that he identified and described could be understood as an economic entity in the way in which he presented it. The difficulty was that Machlup's distinction between knowledge occupations and non-knowledge occupations, real as it was, was only a partial description of the phenomena that he was *not* describing; it was this very trap into which Porat fell in his over-extended definition of the knowledge workforce that Hayes and others subsequently had to correct.[58] Bell made essentially the same error, but it was manifested in a different way. Bell identified the knowledge industry with the service sector, and argued that the post-industrial society was a service-based economy that was knowledge-driven. What he failed to demonstrate was that there was the linear linkage which he implied between these three developments.

Bell's logical lapses, however, are those of an original and inspirational thinker. His work remains central to an understanding of how the concept of the information society has developed. Indeed, whether he was right or wrong, he was immensely influential, for this thesis that post-industrialism, service provision and the knowledge base are symbiotically linked has been the philosophical foundation of much subsequent thinking and writing about the information society. Just as Porat crudely differentiated between the information economy and everything else, Bell differentiated between the traditional industrial economy and everything else. To Bell, what was left, and what was to come, was what we now call the information society. Perhaps the most explicit identification of the 'post-industrial' and the 'information' society is in the work of the Japanese writer, Yoneji Masuda. It is exemplified in the title of his most famous work, *The information society as post-industrial society*, published in 1980.[59]

Other explanations and theories of the information society

There are, however, other and distinctively different explanations and theories of the information society. Bell's model was essentially economic, although he explored social consequences; this explains his reliance on Machlup and his emphasis on the changing structure of industrial capitalism in mid-20th century America. In the early 1960s, the German philosopher Jürgen Habermas developed the concept of

what is called in English the 'public sphere', although the first major
work in which he expounded his theory was not translated into English until 1989.[60] At the core of Habermas's concept of the public
sphere is the metaphor of a common or shared space in which public
opinion can be formed. Hence it encompasses the mass media as well
as interpersonal social interaction. Habermas argues that, paradox-
ically, the public sphere was degraded in the 20th century, despite the
apparent triumph of mass democracy and the importance of the mass
media. The educated and articulate middle classes, he argued, gradually withdrew from the public sphere and became the objects rather
than the subjects of political action. Although Habermas has changed
his views since 1962, and has indeed been intensely criticized by Marx-
ists and feminists, it was in this original form that they had some
impact on the development of the concept of an information society.
Habermas was understood to be arguing that the decline of the public sphere, and the post-modern fragmentation of society, was related
to the growth of the mass media and the instantaneous availability of
so much information through so many channels of communication.

Habermas's Marxian critics were dissatisfied with his analysis of the
mass media. The American sociologist Herbert I. Schiller, in a series
of works from the 1960s to the 1990s,[61] developed an analysis of the
media that effectively presented the information society as being
dominated by the capitalists who controlled the press and the broadcasting networks. He and his colleagues argued that the media's
enthusiasm for the information society, and for the development of
the technologies that sustained it, was largely a product of their own
self-interest. While the Marxian position may now be generally dis-
credited, it had some important consequences, particular in the bur-
geoning academic discipline of media studies in the 1980s. The
application of discourse analysis techniques to the contents of the
media became a significant aspect of sociological activity. In terms of
his theorizing of the information society, Schiller, like Habermas (and
indeed Bell, although from a very different perspective) saw what he
believed to be a sharp break with the past. A new society had been
created on the back of the mass media and the technologies and
economies that sustained them.

The sharp break with the past was not accepted by all theorists of
the information society. The British sociologist Anthony Giddens

argued that it has deep historical roots, and that information has always been a vital component of society. His concern, from a left-of-centre perspective, is that the technologies of information and communications are in danger of creating an over-powerful state.[62] Giddens came to have significant political influence in Britain at the end of the 1990s. He identified himself with New Labour and wrote what amounts to its intellectual manifesto.[63] He did so without any significant reference to information technology or even the media. When he discusses 'public space', he does so in terms of the regeneration of physical spaces such as parks, rather than in terms of Habermas's metaphorical space in which debate takes place and public opinion is formed.[64] Indeed, the social democratic thinking that dominated British politics at the very end of the 20th century seemed void of a coherent concept of the information society. It may be that this reflects Giddens's earlier attachment to the idea (not in itself invalid) that the importance of information in society was nothing new. But technologies had changed, and some more overtly political writers did indeed recognize the potential for electronic extensions of democratic participation.[65] It was only more independent writers, however, who seemed prepared to address the issues that were arising from the consequences of new communications and information technologies, in terms of global media corporations, cross-ownership between the press and the broadcast media, and almost uncontrollable extra-territorial broadcasting.[66]

The British social scientist Frank Webster has discerned a clear distinction between those who believe that the information society is radically new and those who see it as the present manifestation of a long period of continuous and continuing change. He himself inclines to the latter view, writing of what he calls the 'informatisation of life', by which he means the growing awareness of the significance of information and its communication.[67] Nowhere is this view more forcefully expressed than in the recent writings of Manuel Castells. Castells, a one-time Marxist, has written what is probably the most thorough, and certainly the most extensive, analysis of the evolution and present state of the information society.[68] Castells's starting point is that networks have changed everything, and that electronic networking – the internet – has wrought fundamental change. It is never entirely clear whether he sees this change as evolutionary or revolutionary, despite

his long and invaluable historical expositions of social and cultural
trends. Indeed, it may not matter, for his concern is with consequences
as much as it is with causes. He is particularly concerned, perhaps,
with the social impact of change at the most personal level: the individual and the family, the socially included and the socially excluded,
social groups, ethnic and sexual majorities and minorities. His vision
of the future is of the possibility of harmony underpinned by global
economic, social and communications networks. But Castells is no
unthinking advocate of change. He recognizes that information deprivation can lead to the social exclusion of whole cultures and countries, and that a global criminal economy is developing in parallel with
legitimate globalization. He is aware of the potential for the abuse of
the power of the media by the decreasing number of those who control it. And so on. But, his early Marxism abandoned, he takes an
essentially humanistic and optimistic view of what is happening.

The theorists of the information society are a motley crew: economists, sociologists, political scientists. Few, if any, are information scientists. What is clear even from this very brief survey is that
information science has had little or no influence on mainstream
thinking about the information society, and formal information theory perhaps even less. The work of Machlup and Porat provided yet
more empirical data for the information scientists to work with, but
the flow has been almost entirely in one direction. Moreover, the phenomena that the social scientists and economists have been studying
are vastly more extensive than the narrow sphere claimed by information science. Yet it remains the case that information science deals
with the analysis and dissemination of information, and it is common
ground among all the theorists that information is a critical com-
modity to the effective functioning of the economy and of society at
large. Even those who deny that there has been sudden or revolutionary change accept that information is of the highest importance;
differences of opinion revolve around how to explain that phenomenon, and when it can first be observed, rather than in arguing for or
against the existence of the phenomenon itself.

Why has information science played so small a part in this discourse about the changing nature of our society when all those who
participate in the debate agree that information lies at the heart of it?
The answer perhaps lies in part in the narrow intellectual focus of the

discipline, but also in the universality of the technological changes, which even the most conservative of social theorists cannot deny. Communication and information technology, the basis of those electronic networks to which Castells ascribes such massive importance, could never be the sole preserve of any one discipline. Electronic data processing began under the pressure of war, and was developed under the pressure of a tense and potentially fatal armed peace. How it came to dominate the provision of information, and thinking about the information society, is the subject of the next chapter.

A note on further reading

The best introduction to the theorists of the information society, which goes into considerable depth, is Webster (note 12). The author does much more than summarize the work of those about whom he is writing. He has a distinctive view, which we have referred to in this chapter. For those who would like to follow through on some of the primary writings on the information society, the starting point is probably Bell (note 54). Habermas (note 60) is not easy reading, but rewards those who persist. Among the more recent, and more politically committed, Giddens (note 62) has a distinctive view.

There is no obvious introductory work on information theory. Probably the best starting point in Wersig's article on 'Information Theory', in Feather and Sturges (note 27). For the reader whose principal interest is in the information studies dimension of the subject, many of the papers we have cited are essential reading, especially those of Buckland (note 38), Stonier (note 39), and Belkin (note 34). Any serious student of information science, or of any aspect of the social and economic function of information management, should have a first-hand acquaintance with the work of Machlup (note 44), Porat (note 50) and their critics such as Martin (note 51) and Hayes (note 52).

Notes and references

1   *Concise Oxford dictionary*, 9th edn (CD-ROM), Oxford University Press, 1997.
2   *Collins softback English dictionary,* 3rd edn, HarperCollins, 1991.

3 *Concise Oxford dictionary*, 9th edn, 1997.

4 *Collins softback English dictionary*, 3rd edn, 1991.

5 See M. T. Clanchy, *From memory to written record*, Edward Arnold, 1979.

6 Walter J. Ong, *The presence of the word: some prolegomena for cultural and religious history*, Yale University Press, 1967. See also the same author's classic *Orality and literacy: the technologizing of the word*, Routledge, 1982.

7 The classic argument for the significance of the invention of printing is in Elizabeth L. Eistenstein's *The printing press as an agent of change: communications and cultural transformations in early–modern Europe*, Cambridge University Press, 2 vols., 1979. Her hypothesis must now be read, however, in the light of the very important corrective argument in Adrian Johns, *The nature of the book: print and knowledge in the making*, University of Chicago Press, 1998. More generally, and for a different approach, see David R. Olson, *The world on paper: the conceptual and cognitive implications of reading and writing*, Cambridge University Press, 1994.

8 John Locke, *Some thoughts concerning education*, A. and J. Churchill, 1693, p. A2 verso.

9 John Locke, *Two treatises of government*, Awnsham Churchill, 1690.

10 Although developed some years earlier. But the *Two treatises* was not published until after 1688.

11 There is a vast literature. Two useful introductory texts, written for students but thoughtful and scholarly, are: Madan Sarup, *An introductory guide to post-structuralism and postmodernism*, Harvester/Wheatsheaf, 2nd edn, 1993; and Margaret A. Rose, *The post-modern and the post-industrial: a critical analysis*, Cambridge University Press, 1991, 3–20.

12 For this term, in the present context, see Frank Webster, *Theories of the information society*, Routledge, 1995, 138–40.

13 See Rose (note 11), and see also below, pp. 14–15, for a discussion of the views of Daniel Bell, one of the major theorists of post-industrialism.

14 Francis Fukuyama, *The end of history and the last man*, The Free Press, 1992. The original and more polemical version was as an article: The end of history, *The National Interest*, **16**, 1989, 3–18.

15 Jesse H. Shera, Of librarianship, documentation and information science, *UNESCO Bulletin for Libraries*, **22** (2), 1968, 58–65.

16 B. G. Goedegebuure, Celebrating FID's centennial – the Tokyo Resolution, *FID News Bulletin*, **44**, 1994, 115–17.

17 It is now, after several transformations, part of the British Library, and has long since left its original home.

18 For Bradford's own cumulative thoughts, see S. C. Bradford, *Documentation*, Crosby Lockwood, 1948. A full mathematical exposition will be found in B. C. Vickery, Bradford's Law of Scattering, *Journal of Documentation*, **4** (3), 1948, 198–203.

19 For a general account of the historical development of journal literature, the problems it posed and the means by which it was addressed, see Brian Vickery, A century of scientific and technical information, *Journal of Documentation*, **55** (5), 1999, 476–527.

20 Royal Society Scientific Information Conference, 21 June–2 July 1948, *Report and papers submitted*, The Royal Society, 1948. For the background, see Brian Vickery, The Royal Society Scientific Information Conference of 1948, *Journal of Documentation*, **54** (3), 1998, 281–3.

21 J. D. Bernal, *The social function of science*, Routledge, 1939. The most directly relevant comments are on pp. 292–308, but the whole book is still worth reading.

22 D. J. de Solla Price, *Big science, little science*, Columbia University Press, 1963, another classic that has stood the text of time.

23 For example, the Working Party on Mechanical Indexing reported on punch-card sorters, 'a machine to store information on magnetized drums . . . under development by Dr Booth (Birkbeck College [London University])' and on 'The UNIVAC machine [which] stores information electronically and on magnetic tapes' (Royal Society Scientific Information Conference, p. 159). The word *computer* (of which the UNIVAC was of course an early specimen) does not appear in the index.

24 See below, pp. 26–9.

25 Hal Borko, Information science: what is it?, *American Documentation*, **19** (1), 1968, 3–5.

26 By A. J. Meadows in his Introduction to A. J. Meadows (ed.), *The origins of information science*, Taylor Graham/Institute of Information Scientists, 1987, 1.

27 R. T. Bottle, Information Science. In John Feather and Paul Sturges (eds), *International encyclopaedia of information and library science*, Routledge, 1997, 212.

28 Gernot Wersig, Information science: the study of postmodern knowledge use, *Information Processing and Management*, **29**, 1993, 229–39.

29 Bottle, 213.

30 Claude E. Shannon, A mathematical theory of communication, *Bell Systems Technical Journal*, **27**, 1948, 379–423, 623–58. This is the original publication of his work in its most scientific form.

31 Claude E. Shannon and Warren Weaver, *The mathematical theory of communication*, University of Illinois Press, 1949.

32 Indeed, we use it in this way in Chapter 3.

33 See the analysis in Charles Cole, Shannon revisited: information in terms of uncertainty. *Journal of the American Society of Information Science*, **4** (4), 1993, 204–11. Cole detected an internal inconsistency in Shannon's own work, which in his view allowed information scientists to use it in their own (also conflicting) ways.

34 Nick Belkin, The cognitive viewpoint in information science, *Journal of Information Science*, **16**, 1990, 11–15.

35 Norbert Wiener, *Cybernetics, or control and communication in the animal and the machine*, 2nd edn, MIT Press, 1961. The first edition was published in 1948.

36 See below, pp. 15–17.

37 See above, p. 7.

38 Michael Buckland, *Information and information systems*, Greenwood Press, 1991, 41–52. For a detailed analysis, see Michael K. Buckland, Information as thing, *Journal of the American Society of Information Science*, **42** (5), 1991, 351–60.

39 Tom Stonier, Towards a new theory of information, *Journal of Information Science*, **17** (5), 1991, 257–63.

40 Buckland, Information as thing, 354–5.

41 See, for example, Raul Luciano Katz, *The information society: an international perspective*, Praeger, 1988, 1, and the sources cited in

note 1 there.

42 See A. S. Duff, Daniel Bell's theory of the information society, *Journal of Information Science*, **24** (6), 1998, 373–94.

43 On Machlup, see J. S. Dryer (ed.), *Breadth and depth in economics: Fritz Machlup – the man and his ideas*, D. C. Heath, 1978.

44 Fritz Machlup, *The production and distribution of knowledge in the United States*, Princeton University Press, 1962.

45 David Landes, *The wealth and poverty of nations: why some are so rich and some so poor*, Abacus, 1998, 459–61.

46 See Paul Kennedy, *The rise and fall of the great powers: economic change and military conflict from 1500 to 1800*, Fontana, 1989, 455–6, which deals specifically with aircraft production. But the whole chapter of which this is a part (pp. 447–564) is relevant.

47 Landes, 480–90.

48 Table 1.1 is derived (and greatly simplified), from Machlup's Table X-3 on pp. 384–5.

49 Machlup, 382–7.

50 Marc U. Porat, *The information economy: definition and measurement*, US Dept of Commerce, Office of Telecommunications, 1977.

51 See William J. Martin, *The global information society*, Aslib/Gower, 1995, 95–9.

52 See Robert M. Hayes, A simplified model for the infrastructure of national information economies. In *Proceedings of the NIT '92 conference, Hong Kong, 30 November–2 December 1992*. For international comparisons, see Katz, p. 8, Table 1.1, and p. 19, Table 1.7.

53 'I propose that we get rid of the duplication "knowledge and information" . . . we may occasionally refer to certain kinds of knowledge as "information", but we shall avoid the redundant phrase "knowledge *and* information"' (Machlup, p. 8).

54 Daniel Bell, *The coming of a post-industrial society: a venture in social forecasting*, Heinemann, 1974, 9.

55 Duff, 376.

56 Bell, 202–5.

57 This is the essence of Duff's argument.

58 See above.

59 Yoneji Masuda, *The information society as post-industrial society*, Institute for the Information Society, 1980. A revised edition was published as *Managing in the information society: releasing synergy Japanese style*, Basil Blackwell, 1990. Masuda was an innovative participant in the informatization of Japan, as well as being an astute observer of the process in which he was playing a leading role.

60 Jürgen Habermas, *Strukturwandel der Öffenlichkeit*, Luchterhand, 1962; 2nd edn, Suhrkamp, 1989. Translated as *The structural transformation of the public sphere*, Polity Press, 1989. Habermas is a major figure in philosophy, whose work has spawned a large expository literature. We are particularly indebted to William Outhwaite, *Habermas: a critical introduction*, Polity Press, 1994.

61 See Webster, 74 ff., for an account of Schiller's work. Schiller's own position is perhaps most accessible in his *Information and the crisis economy*, Ablex, 1984, and in its most developed form in Herbert Schiller et al., *The ideology of international communications*, Institute for Media Analysis, 1992.

62 Anthony Giddens, *Social theory and modern sociology*, Polity Press, 1987.

63 Anthony Giddens, *The third way: the renewal of social democracy*, Polity Press, 1998.

64 For example, Giddens, *Third way*, 107–8.

65 Peter Mandelson and Roger Liddle, *The Blair revolution: can New Labour deliver?*, Faber and Faber, 1996, 208–9.

66 See, for example, Will Hutton, *The state we're in*, Vintage, revised edn, 1996, 219–23. Hutton, a journalist, was at that time a public supporter of New Labour.

67 Webster, 216–20; the phrase is on p. 218.

68 Manuel Castells, *The rise of the network society*, Blackwell, 1996; *The power of identity*, Blackwell, 1997; *End of millennium*, Blackwell, 1998. The three together constitute a single work under the general title *The information age: economy, society and culture*.

2

A new technology
for information

Introduction

Information technology had become so commonplace by the turn of
the 21st century that we have perhaps already forgotten how recently
it has been developed. Some of the most familiar applications – most
obviously the world wide web – were less than a decade old in the
year 2000. Technologies that can process and transmit information
have become central to many aspects of life, and have come to dominate some of the thinking about the information society. We should
not, however, fall into the trap of supposing either that information
technology defines the information society or that the information
society is nothing but computing and associated activities such as the
internet. Moreover, we must recognize that information storage and
processing devices, and devices for the communication of information are different. Their convergence, a critical moment in the history
of both, is comparatively recent.

Communications technologies have existed for far longer than
those for information storage and processing. Telegraphy, telephony
and wireless transmission are all inventions of the 19th century, and
radio and television broadcasting of the early 20th century. There
were over a million telephones in the USA before 1900.[1] International
telephone networks existed before World War 1, radio broadcasting
was all but universal before World War 2, and television was in most
homes in the developed world long before any home had its own
computer.[2] Despite all these caveats, however, we would not wish to

deny the broad accuracy of the widespread perception that computers and computer networks have had a very important role in driving forward the information society, and that they are now central to understanding its operation. In this chapter we shall consider some aspects of their history and development as the basis of a consideration of the role which they play now and may play in the future.

Computers

Early computers

The early analysts of the development of the knowledge-driven economy, and the first prophets of the information society, were working in the late 1940s and early 1950s when the potential of electronic data processing was only beginning to be imagined. The first electronic computer to be revealed to the public was ENIAC, an American machine built in 1946. This is the moment that is generally taken to mark the beginning of public awareness of the new invention.[3] There was, of course, a long history behind this event. A machine that could make, or could assist in making, calculations had long been regarded as a *desideratum* by scientists and engineers, and indeed for more mundane purposes. The abacus was one such device; the slide rule was another. But developing a machine that could perform calculations automatically – and by implication without the errors that are the inevitable consequence of human intervention – remained a long-term goal. Many mathematicians contributed to the conceptualization of a calculating machine, but it was the Englishman Charles Babbage who came closest to solving the problem. Indeed, it is now conventional to regard Babbage as the intellectual progenitor of the computer.[4] Babbage never built his 'analytical engine', as he called it, although one was successfully built recently at the Science Museum in London, following his designs.

Babbage's analytical engine contained all the essential elements of a computer: there was an input device for both data and programs (on punch cards), there was a processing unit where the calculations were made (Babbage called this the 'mill'), and there was a memory with random access from which data could be retrieved and in which intermediate results could be stored during processing (the 'store').

There was also to be a printing device for output. Although Babbage's engine was not built at the time, other less sophisticated devices were; as a result, by the first half of the 20th century mechanical calculators were familiar in businesses and among mathematicians and others using numbers as part of their work. Mechanical calculation, however, was only one part of Babbage's concept; the intellectually central element was the capacity of the analytical engine to be pre-programmed and to store and retrieve information. It was this concept that was revived during World War 2 in an attempt to speed up essential war work.

Bletchley Park and Alan Turing

The story of the secret British activities at Bletchley Park has gradually been revealed since the mid-1970s. The intense secrecy which surrounded it, long after the end of the War, deprived those who worked there of their rightful claim to be among the inventors of the electronic computer. Only now is the record being set straight.[5]

Bletchley Park was the centre of British cryptanalysis; its staff were required to decipher the codes used by the Germans for their wireless traffic. A team of scientists, engineers, mathematicians and non-specialists with suitably recondite minds was set to work. Their principal target was the codes generated by a machine called ENIGMA. This was a purely mechanical device that encoded and decoded wireless messages by using cogwheels; a daily 'key' was used to set the machine, which then generated codes which could only be broken by identifying that day's key.[6] Through a combination of using captured German machines, drawing on the work of pre-War Polish and French cryptanalysts, making their own brilliant deductions and sheer hard work, the British team mastered the principles of ENIGMA and cracked the codes almost daily. Nevertheless, the process was slow, and the members of the team were continually looking for better ways of achieving their ends. The essence of the problem was to find a means of almost instantaneously collating vast amounts of data by looking for patterns in seemingly random combinations of letters. It was an exercise in logical data processing.

In conceptual terms, this was already understood by at least one member of the Bletchley Park team, Alan Turing. He was a math-

ematician who, before the War, had published a number of papers
dealing with some of the most esoteric, yet fundamental, problems of
pure mathematics.[7] In the course of his work, Turing followed
through the internal logic of a subject that was essentially dependent
upon mechanistic logical progression, and in a paper of 1936 imagined a machine that would undertake the calculations.[8] At the time,
no such machine could be built, but under the pressure of war the
idea was revived and turned into reality. The wartime work brought
together the mathematicians and the electrical engineers; it was from
that union that the computer was born. The Bletchley Park team
worked with Post Office telephone engineers to build the device that
Turing had conceptualized; the engineer principally responsible was
Tommy Flowers, who has been even more neglected than Turing himself in the history of computing.[9] The first machine to be built, which
contained some 1500 valves at its electronic core, was called the
'Heath Robinson' in tribute to a contemporary cartoonist who was
known for the fantastic devices in his comic drawings. Despite its
name, it worked. Indeed, although doubts persisted among both the
scientists and the military, Heath Robinson worked well enough to be
developed further. The result was Colossus, which became operational at the end of 1943. Turing and Flowers had built a program-
mable data processor, which was a computer in all but name.

The obsessive secrecy with which the British shrouded Bletchley
Park's work, even after the end of the War, allowed the initiative to
pass to the USA where it has largely remained ever since. The subsequent development of computers was at once rapid and fitful. Teams
in the USA and Britain, in universities, in industry, and in the military and espionage communities, worked both in competition and in
partnership to develop larger, faster and more powerful machines.
But it was at least a decade before their significance began to be perceived outside scientific circles, and longer than that before policy
makers and politicians understood their long-term implications. As
we have seen, the 1948 Royal Society conference on scientific information did identify some possible uses for these new devices (which
few of the participants even in that conference can ever have seen),
but that is a rare early example of a suggestion that computers might
be used to assist in the storage, management and dissemination of
non-numerical data.[10]

Computers in the 1950s and 1960s

Throughout the 1950s and into the 1960s, computers were essentially tools for scientists. They were physically huge, massively expensive and could only be operated by those with specialist knowledge. They were to be found in government and university research laboratories, especially in those which had the resources which at that time were associated with defence-related research. The banks and insurance companies also began to take an interest in the 1950s, following the pioneering lead of the Bank of America, which bought its first computer in 1953.[11] Despite this comparatively slow start (as it now seems), development was continuous. In centres like the University of Manchester in Britain (where Turing worked until his suicide in 1954) and, above all, at the Massachusetts Institute of Technology in the USA, work went on apace. The MIT Computer Science Laboratory was a particular hotbed of activity.[12] Among those who worked there were Wiener, the founder of cybernetics, and John von Neumann, another German–American mathematician who contributed much of the basic work on logic, memory and random access. By the end of the 1950s, the mainframes (as they subsequently came to be called) were capable of working with large quantities of data, and their potential for application outside the world of numerical data processing was becoming clear.[13] During the 1960s and 1970s, computers became smaller, quicker and cheaper, although at the time it was not clear that this was what was actually happening. Indeed, it was during these early decades of their use that computers acquired their reputation for unreliability. 'The computer made a mistake' became a common cry across Europe and the USA. Of course, sometimes it did. Like any machine a computer can malfunction. But, more often, the error was a human one in programming, input or operation. Nevertheless, the public perception that computers were less reliable than people became widespread, and residually survives today.

Networks

In computing itself, the great development of the 1960s was the invention and application of two key technologies: the transistor and the integrated circuit. Together they permitted the development of the microcomputer, as it was initially called, the immediate forerunner of the ubiquitous Personal Computer of the end of the century.[14] Applications of computing became commonplace in many offices. Word processing had all but ousted traditional typewriting in the industrialized countries by the late 1980s. Computers were making their way into the home as both toys and tools. No-one born in the developed world after about 1980 can remember life without them. By the mid-1990s, 35% of all US households had a computer;[15] this represented about 10 million machines. By 1996, the figure had risen to about 22 million.[16]

The development of computers, however, is only one part of the story. The other, and in some ways more important, part is the development of communications systems that allowed machines to work together rather than separately. There were of course electric communications networks in existence long before the invention of computers – the telegraph and the telephone – as well as wireless networks used for the transmission of radio and television signals and broadcasts. From the early years of computing, there were those who began to conceptualize a network that linked computers. The person who probably had the greatest long-term influence on this vital development was Paul Baran, an American electronics engineer who, after a shaky start in computing and television in the late 1940s and early 1950s, went to California to work for the RAND Corporation, a prototype think tank organization. At RAND, he was encouraged to develop his ideas about networks, eventually conceptualizing the notion of subdividing information into small packets, which could then be transmitted through telecommunications networks between computers. The idea came from Baran's increasing familiarity with information theory, and the notion that information was an entity that could be described, analysed and processed. The telecommunications companies were suspicious to the point of hostility, but the military were very interested indeed. The Advanced Research Projects Agency (ARPA) had the nuclear defence of the USA at the top of its agenda. Its computer scientists came across Baran's work, and commissioned him to look at its defence potential.[17] In October 1969, working with the University of California at Los Angeles (UCLA), ARPANET successfully established a network initially linking four academic computing sites, an event now regarded as the moment when the internet began.[18] Developments in the UK and France followed within a year, and international networking came shortly afterwards.[19]

Networking outside the defence community remained an academic tool – some at the time might have said toy – until the late 1970s, when the potential of PCs was beginning to be recognized. The National Science Foundation in the USA, the sponsor of much of the science that had created ARPANET, agreed in 1979 to allow commercial exploitation of the network, a challenge taken up first by the establishment of CompuServe, and then by that of the rival America Online (AOL).[20] The underpinning technologies were now in place. PCs could be linked to the common carrier telecommunications networks through modems, and there were protocols that regulated such matters as file transfer, electronic mail addresses and the packet switching systems. Throughout the 1980s, the internet grew steadily, although largely within the scientific and academic communities. Users still needed considerable skill in the use of computers. Telecommunications links were not always reliable, and were often slow. What was needed was a simple, universally understood, interface that would allow non-expert users to access the net and all that that implied.

The world wide web

The solution was, of course, the world wide web. The story of the web is now well known, and has been recounted by, among others, its inventor, the English physicist, Tim Berners-Lee.[21] Berners-Lee was working at CERN, the European particle physics research centre in Geneva, and set himself the task of devising a system that would capture the information held by CERN's large transient population of visiting scientists as well as by its own staff. The system that he developed was based on the use of hypermedia. Hypermedia had been first conceptualized in the 1930s by an American electrical engineer, Vannevar Bush, who devised a machine capable of linking 'trails' of information, which could be stored and retrieved at a later date. Bush's ideas remained unpublished until 1945, when he used an article in *Atlantic Monthly* to described a machine capable of storing and retrieving data.[22] This machine – the Memex[23] – was a mechanized desk-sized storage device that allowed the reader to create associative links between publications stored on microfilm via two screens and a mechanical keyboard. Bush's concept was based on the observation that we do not always read a document in a strictly linear way: we move from text to footnote, for example, or abandon one text to consult another, or move between text and illustration; we use indexes and tables of contents; and we simply browse. Hypermedia was an attempt to reproduce this natural human approach to information gathering in an electronic environment.

The Memex, like Babbage's analytical engine before it, was in fact never built. The concept of associative computing, and computing that was designed to supplement human cognitive function (rather than *replacing* cognitive function) was, however, developed further in the 1960s. In 1963, the American academic Douglas Englebart's Augmentation Research Center started development of NLS (oNLine System), which aimed to produce a visual computing system that would allow the sharing of information via networks.[24] The NLS project was responsible for successfully developing the computer mouse (patented in 1967), e-mail, word processing and the first working hypermedia system (demonstrated in 1968)[25] and effectively pioneered techniques and methods of working that are ubiquitous at the start of the 21st century.

The concept of hypermedia, aided by the development of the first networks (called in the early 1970s 'internetting', and hence the foreshortened 'internet'), was supplemented by the work of Ted Nelson. It was Nelson who coined the phrase 'hypertext' in 1965. The development of his idea of what he called the 'docuverse', which he defined as a 'hypertext publishing network' containing all human knowledge, was to become his life work. While Nelson's influence on the development of hypertext should not be underestimated, the docuverse (known more commonly as Xanadu) never materialized despite the announcement of its impending arrival in 1974.[26] Despite commercial backing for Xanadu in 1988, and indications that it would be available in 1992, Nelson's concept still remains unrealized. The real significance of all of this lies in the fact that Bush, Englebart and Nelson shared a vision of computing applications driven by associative thinking, and a vision of computers supplementing human knowledge rather than supplanting human knowledge. Ironically, Nelson, writing in 1982, overestimated the time scale for hypertext to become the dominant information medium:

Forty years from now (if the human species survives), there will be hundreds of thousands of files servers. And there will be hundreds of millions of simultaneous users. All this is manifest destiny. There is no point in arguing it, either you see it or you don't. [27]

Hypertext worked, and was beginning to be used in some networked applications by the early 1980s.[28] Moreover, the hypermedia concept was readily adaptable to data that was not alphanumeric; the PCs of the late 1980s increasingly had a multimedia capability, and hypertext suited them well.

For Berners-Lee, hypertext provided the ideal medium for his new information system. Because it was driven by the way people work rather than by the way computers work, it allowed him to devise a system that was at once logical and fuzzy. The ability to switch between documents could, in a networked environment, easily be transformed into the ability to switch between different computers. The familiar framework and language of the web emerged rapidly: servers, sites, search engines and so on.[29] The web took off dramatically. It was launched in 1992. When the Mosaic browser became available in 1993, it proved to be the ideal interface, and provided the final-stage booster for Berners-Lee's electronic rocket.[30]

The ease of use of the web is almost equalled by the simplicity of contributing to it. By 1998, there were about 30 million host sites on the internet, the majority of them using the web; this number appears almost to have doubled in the previous two years.[31] In the year 2000, it was estimated that 146.4 million people in the world had access to the internet at home and 34.8 million at work.[32] Of these potential users, nearly 90 million accessed the internet from home in a single month, and, in the same month, 33 million did so from work.[33] To many people, the web – more than anything that has gone before – is the symbol and the triumph of the information age.

A new age?

The web has made it easy to use the internet as a means of seeking and finding information, among many other things. The great increases in net usage as a whole has largely been driven by the web, although the still growing use of electronic mail has also played a part

in this. The formerly esoteric world of computing and networks has
been opened up to millions of people who neither know nor care
what happens inside the machine that sits in front of them. It is as
irrelevant to the average user as is the working of a cathode ray tube
to a television viewer or the principles of carburation to the average
car driver. In the industrialized world, the computer has become
ubiquitous and universal. Is this, then, the information society that
some social prophets have foreseen?

The answer to this question has to be formulated in the light of
some of the paradoxes that we began to explore in Chapter 1. The
argument that the effective functioning of any human society has
always been dependent on knowledge and information is a powerful
one. The argument that the most advanced economies have moved
from an almost total dependence on manufacturing and mineral
extraction for wealth generation to a greater dependence of knowledge-based activities is manifestly true, even if the timing, extent and
radical nature of this change may be more debatable. The issue is
whether these two analyses taken together underpin the case that the
outcome of the social and economic change that has taken place is
indeed an *information* society. This might be dismissed as mere academic wordplay, but its real significance becomes apparent when we
consider a third strand in the argument. This is the contention that
technology has driven the process, and that it is information and
communications technology that provides the link between the
knowledge-based society and the post-industrial society and which
therefore underpins the changes that we now see all around us. Most
commentators reject this technological determinism in its crudest
form,[34] but clearly there is one undeniable element of truth: the
applications of computing, and particularly of networked computing,
have changed the way in which we live and work.

Despite its vastness and complexity, the internet is a very personal
and private medium, quite unlike the one-to-many model of the
broadcast media.[35] It facilitates interpersonal communication
through e-mail, and conversations and conferences through discussion groups and the like (which may be completely open or restricted
to members), as well as providing one-to-many access to information,
largely through websites. Even when it does operate in a one-to-many
model, however, the internet has a capacity that distinguishes it

fundamentally from the other mass media – it is always potentially interactive. It is this capacity for interactivity that really underlies the social and economic change which it is bring in its wake.

The most obvious example of this is in electronic business, e-commerce. The internet was created as a scientific tool, but its release into the public domain at a very early point in its development probably made its full commercialization almost inevitable.[36] The internet as it exists in the early 21st century is largely dependent on private sector funding. Websites are sustained by paid-for advertising; in turn that advertising generates revenue for the advertisers through the sale of their goods and services. Buying and selling over the net is becoming increasingly common, although it still comprises a comparatively small percentage of all transactions; so too is access to financial services. The evidence lies in every advertisement in any medium, with the advertiser's website address prominently displayed.

The same phenomenon is beginning to be seen in the provision of professional services such as those of doctors and lawyers. Net-based education and training, both in the public and the private sectors (where they can still be distinguished from each other) is facilitating the lifelong learning, re-skilling and access to information which are themselves necessary because of the very developments that we are discussing. Two British examples will exemplify this. The so-called University for Industry (UfI) is in effect a virtual learning network accessed through a combination of local study centres and networked electronic learning materials. Marketed under the brand name of LearnDirect, its website provides the first point of access and a complex range of choice for potential learners.[37] A second example is that of the National Health Service, whose NHS Direct site, although far from fully developed, seems likely to become a first point of call for consumer health information of all kinds, and will perhaps relieve medical professionals of some of the pressures they face at present.[38]

Information and communications technologies have never been socially neutral. Since the late 19th century, a succession of inventions has transformed social life, and the way in which business is transacted. The telephone and television, to look no further, exemplify the impact of change. Networked computing, both in the home and in the workplace, are clearly having a comparable impact. Like earlier technologies, however, computing continues to develop. These developments are not only making computers themselves more reliable, more efficient and (in real terms) cheaper; they are also propelling further change in existing technologies. The interface between telephony, broadcasting and computing illustrates this dramatically. The networks that provide access to the internet are, for the vast majority of users, the same networks that provide access to voice telephony. Increasingly, these same cables are being used for the delivery of broadcast television and radio. At the same time, mobile telephony, dependent on microwave radio networks, is beginning to be used as means of access to the internet. The next generation of mobile phones will almost certainly complete the circle. The phenomenal growth of mobile telephony in the 1990s, and statistics suggesting that over half the UK population owned a mobile telephone in November 2000,[39] attest to its popularity. However, the ubiquity of mobile telephones in modern society has not brought automatic success to every venture – Wireless Application Protocol (WAP) phones, offering internet access, failed to reach levels of penetration that the advertising hype predicted in 2000. Additionally, the mixed success of e-commerce business at the turn of the millennium did not spare players in the mobile telecommunications sector, with BT Wireless reportedly under severe financial pressure in early 2001.[40]

Mobile telephony

Like computing, the technology that was ultimately to enable mobile telephony was developed immediately after World War 2. The first 'mobile phone' was demonstrated in the USA by Bell Laboratories in 1946. Commercial development of 'cellular' networks by Bell, from the late 1960s onwards, paved the way for the services we enjoy today, with first generation ('1G') commercial cellular services being offered in Scandinavia in 1981. Subsequently, similar analogue systems were introduced in the USA (Advanced Mobile Phone Service – AMPS), with other countries adopting the same standard. However, generic analogue developments effectively meant some networks were incompatible with each other – for example the UK's Total Access Communication System (TACS). Of course, there were problems. The use of different protocols by players in the young mobile telephony sector threatened the viability of the industry as a whole. Work in the

European Union in the late 1980s centred on developing a broad industry specification, which became the Global System for Mobile Communication (GSM).[41] This specification was developed as a digital service following comparative studies of analogue and digital networks. Digital networks proved to be more efficient than analogue networks, notably in terms of network capacity, call quality and geographical coverage. Development of second-generation ('2G') mobile telephones, and the introduction of commercial services in 1991, transformed the mobile phone industry. As with analogue systems, differing standards (GSM in Europe and Digital-AMPS in North America) effectively blocked network compatibility in some regions, and created problems for 'roaming'.[42] Despite this, however, 2G systems provided the platform for boom in the mobile telecommunications sector. The GSM standard incorporated a range of services that have proved very popular, including data services such as text messaging via the Short Messaging Service (SMS),[43] and voice mail.

Convergence of ICT technologies

The next advance for the mobile telecommunications market was to be the marriage between mobile phones and the internet. During 1997 development started on a platform capable of combining voice communication and internet functionality, known as Wireless Application Protocol (WAP). WAP (sometimes called '2.5G', alluding to it as an early combination of the existing 2G functionality with the predicted future functionality of 3G) allowed the user to browse the 'internet' via the device, but only for pages that were coded in WML (Wireless Mark-up Language). Launched in January 2000 after three years under development, WAP was a commercial disappointment. The reasons for this probably had much to do with misleading advertising, inflated expectations and the slow speed of downloading pages onto the devices when compared with conventional browsing on networked computers. Although WAP was undoubtedly a technical breakthrough, slow uptake of the technology provided early warnings to the telecommunications industry on the pitfalls of introducing new technology to a competitive market. However, it is apparent that the industry views development and investment in Wideband Code Division Multiple Access (W-CDMA) technology as essential. In 2000, five telecommunications companies bid £23 billion between them for five licences to run CDMA ('3G') services in the UK.[44] The vast amount of money invested in the licences provides an accurate reflection of the importance attached by telecommunication companies to the synergy of ICT with 3G technology, and to ICT that can properly be described as 'mobile'. However, the financial burden on these companies also raised concerns about their long-term viability and the eventual price of the 3G devices when they are available for purchase. Whatever the makeup of the telecommunication sector, or the initial prices of equipment, it is evident that we stand on the threshold of an ICT development that will continue the process of fundamental change in how we live and work.

The convergence of ICT technologies is not a new phenomenon, but it is beginning to have consequences that were not – and perhaps could not have been – foreseen. Like any technology, there is nothing intrinsically beneficent or malevolent in the internet. How it is used, and the consequences of use, is a matter for users not providers and certainly not for inventors. It is no more logical to blame Berners-Lee for the dissemination of child pornography on the web than it is to blame Rutherford for Hiroshima. How society uses inventions is a matter to be determined through whatever mechanisms have been put in place for taking decisions about social policy. The problem confronting those with policy-making responsibilities – ultimately national governments and inter-governmental transnational bodies – is the speed at which radical technological innovation is now taking place. The converged technologies for the communication of information, whether across hard-wired or broadcast networks or (as is increasingly common) through some combination of the two, are simply not constrained by politically defined boundaries between nations or social groups. Governments are being forced to wrestle with massive issues of which they not only have little experience (but who has, when so much is new?) and, more significantly, over which they have a diminishing degree of control. In Chapter 4 we shall return to some of the key issues of information policy after we have given further consideration to the practicalities of communications systems.

A note on further reading

The best recent book on the subjects covered in this chapter is Winston (note 2). It is both historically and technologically literate, and takes a rational view of the impact of new technologies and new media on society. Some of the same ground is covered by Naughton (note 18), although that focuses more on the development of computing and the internet. Naughton serves as a good historical introduction to the subjects it covers; a more technical account (somewhat blinkered by its status as an official institutional history) is Garfinkel (note 12). Berners-Lee's autobiographical history (note 21) is a fascinating insight into one of the great original minds of his generation. Finally, Baldwin, McVoy and Steinfeld (note 15) is invaluable as a non-technical account of technical issues, written primarily for media studies students but equally useful for students of information studies.

Notes and references

1   Carolyn Marvin, *When old technologies were new: thinking about electric communication in the late nineteenth century*, Oxford University Press, 1988, 64.
2   See Brian Winston, *Media, technology and society. A history: from the telegraph to the Internet*, Routledge, 1998.
3   Winston, 166–70.
4   A. Hyman, *Charles Babbage: pioneer of the computer*, Oxford University Press, 1984, 164–73, 254–5. Note the subtitle!
5   The latest batch of papers to be released by the Public Record Office leaves no doubt that computers were designed and built at Bletchley Park, and that they were in use before ENIAC was conceived. See Kim Sengupta, GCHQ releases the secret details of how Bletchley Park built the first computer, *Independent*, 30 September 2000, 13. The story of Bletchley Park only began to come into the public domain in the 1970s with the publication of F. W. Winterbotham, *The Ultra secret*, Weidenfeld and Nicolson, 1974. See also, for a readable recent account, Singh, S., *The code book: the secret history of codes and codebreaking*, Fourth Estate, 2000, 143–89.
6   For the operation of ENIGMA, see S. Singh, 124–42.
7   For Turing, see A. Hodges, *Alan Turing, the enigma*, Simon and

Schuster, 1983, which is a fine account of the man and of his work. See also **http://www.turing.org.uk/turing**, an excellent website edited by Hodges.

8 Alan Turing, On computable numbers, with an application to the *Entscheidungsproblem, Proceedings of the London Mathematical Society*, **42**, 1936, 230–65. For our purposes, it is (fortunately for us) unnecessary to understand the mathematical issues; the point is Turing's recognition of the possibility of designing a machine that could do the mechanical part of the work once the problem had been formulated and a methodology devised for solving it.

9 There are of course references to him in the literature, but they tend to downplay his role; without him there would have been no Heath Robinson and no Colossus. See, for example, Winston, 173; the balance is somewhat redressed in the article in the *Independent* in note 5 above.

10 See above, p. 6.

11 Winston, 205.

12 Simson L. Garfinkel, *Architects of the information society: thirty-five years of the Laboratory for Computer Science at MIT*, MIT Press, 1999.

13 The delay in identifying what a new technology can do best is a well-known phenomenon in the history of science. For some anecdotes about early telephone usage, see Marvin, Chapters 2 and 3. The same theme is the central hypothesis of Winston.

14 Winston, 206–40.

15 Thomas F. Baldwin, D. Stevens McVoy and Charles Steinfeld, *Convergence: integrating media, information and communication*, Sage Publications, 1996, 59, 149.

16 Reliable absolutely current data is difficult to find. These figures are based on M. Tawfik (ed.), *World communication and information report 1999–2000*, UNESCO, 2000, Figure A5. This document is also available at
http://www.unesco.org/webworld/wcir/en.html
It should be noted, however, that data are often contradictory. We have tried to maintain a degree of consistency in this minefield by only directly comparing data that come from similar sources, so that at least the *comparison* is reasonably robust.

17 This is not always made clear in the literature. See, however,

Jerry Everard, *Virtual states: the internet and the boundaries of the nation state*, Routledge, 2000, 12–13. Baran's report (from 1964) has been reproduced on the web at **http://www.rand.org/publications/RM/RM.3420/**

18 See Winston, 328–9; and the less technical account in John Naughton, *A brief history of the future: the origins of the internet*, Weidenfeld & Nicolson, 1999, 117.

19 Everard, 14–16.

20 Winston, 333.

21 Tim Berners-Lee, *Weaving the web: the past, present and future of the world wide web*, Orion Business Books, 1999. See also Naughton, 209–52.

22 Vannevar Bush, As we may think, *Atlantic Monthly*, **176**, 1945, 101–8.

23 A downloadable animation of how Memex was designed to work can be found at **http://www.dynamicdiagrams.com/design/memex/model.htm**

24 For further information on Englebart's career, see **http://www.bootstrap.org/dce-bio.htm**

25 RealVideo footage of Englebart's 90-minute demonstration of NLS at Stanford University is available at **http://sloan.stanford.edu/MouseSite/1968Demo.html**

26 Ted Nelson, *Computer lib*, rev. edn, Tempus Books, 1987.

27 Ted Nelson, Miracle device: Feed's document on Ted Nelson's literary machines, *Feed Magazine*, January 1998, available at **http://www.feedmag.com/templates/old_article.php3?a_id=1210** This article is based on Ted Nelson, *Literary machines*, Mindful Press, 1982.

28 Naughton, 218–21.

29 For further discussion of the web as a communications system, see below, pp. 46–51.

30 Berners-Lee, 75–80; Naughton, 243–6.

31 Tawfik, comparing Table A1 (which shows 16.2 million hosts in 1996) and Figure 12.9, which shows an estimated 30 million in January 1998). We deal with some of the implications of this in Chapter 4, pp. 60–1 below.

32 Of course, there is very substantial overlap between these two groups.

33　August 2000 internet usage statistics available at
**http://cyberatlas.internet.com/big_picture/traffic_patterns/
article/0,,5931_465241,00.html**

34　As do we; see above, pp. 25–6.

35　We pursue in the context of the Shannon and Weaver model in
Chapter 3, pp. 46–7.

36　See above, p. 31.

37　**http://www.learndirect.co.uk**

38　**http://www.nhsdirect.nhs.uk**

39　A range of statistics on mobile usage can be found at *Cellular
Online* at
http://www.cellular.co.za
For statistics for the UK and Ireland, see
http://www.cellular.co.za/stats/stats-uk-irish-gsm-networks.htm

40　Reuters, BT slips to three-year lows, available at
http://news.zdnet.co.uk/story/0,,s2085171,00.html

41　For further detail, see John Scourias, *Overview of the Global System for Mobile Communications*, at
**http://www.shoshin.uwaterloo.ca/~jscouria/GSM/gsmreport.
html**

42　'Roaming' is the name for the facility that allows a phone user
to use compatible networks in countries other than that in
which it is registered. Development of GSM allowed 'roaming' in
Europe from the early 1990s.

43　The Short Messaging Service (SMS) allows the user to send
alphanumeric messages (with a maximum of 160 characters) to
other users. SMS has become a very popular function, with a
reported 9 billion text messages sent worldwide in August 2000
alone. There are also indications that the SMS function is now
almost as popular as using the devices to speak to people. See
Nine billion g-mails per month, new world record for wireless text, 26
November 2000, at
**http://www.cellular.co.za/news_2000/news-11262000_nine_
billion_sms.htm**

44　W-CDMA networks are more commonly known in Europe as
UMTS (Universal Mobile Telephony System) and in Japan as
FOMA (Freedom of Mobile Multimedia Access).

3

The flow of information

Introduction

The economic structure of the modern world is argued to be dependent on information. In Chapter 1, we explored various theories – historical, sociological, economic, political – that try to explain the extent to which that is true, and how and why it has come about. Some commentators go further and make either predictions or prescriptions for the future. Some set social and economic goals, and suggest political actions that would allow those goals to be achieved. Others take a view that future developments are inevitable, and can be only marginally influenced. While there is a general sense of being different from the past, there are also very divergent views about what constitutes that difference and what its effects have been, are and will be.

All agree that information technology has important implications for the way in which the global economy works, and hence for political and social structures internationally, nationally and regionally. Some argue, with Castells, that the informatization of society and the development of information systems and networks represents a fundamental shift in the parameters of human existence. Others, with Webster and Giddens, reject this technological determinism by arguing that technological change, however innovative, does not itself drive societal change but is merely one aspect of it. No one, however, denies that information technology has had a profound impact, if only in emphasizing the importance of the issues that are being discussed. It has revolutionized communications, has induced major changes in economic activity, has begun to influence the way in which we educate our children, and has made a difference to how we conduct our social lives. This is not a determinist view; it merely acknowledges observable facts.

In this chapter we shall explore further some of the technological mechanisms that are argued to underpin our contemporary information society, and some of the issues that arise out of their development and use. We shall first try to define what is perceived as being so different, developing some of the themes that have emerged in Chapters 1 and 2. We shall then explore a little further some of the technologies themselves. Finally we shall look at the information that is being distributed and used.

The old and the new

Technology can be linked with information in two ways: it can be used to store it, and to communicate it. To take a simple example, we can store data on the hard disc of a PC; we can communicate that data across a network to another PC. The basic technology of the two processes is the same, since both depend on the ability to create, store and retrieve digital data. The communication of the information, as we saw in considering the Shannon and Weaver model,[1] depends on the compatibility of two ends of a system that links the source with the receiver. The fact that Shannon and Weaver developed the theory before there were computers that could communicate with each other electronically merely strengthens their claim to having enunciated a valid general theory.

The Shannon and Weaver model is clearly applicable to the various electrical communications systems developed during the 19th century, which were its original exemplars, such as telegraphy and telephony. One recent writer has described the electric telegraph as 'the Victorian internet'.[2] This is more than just a catchy book title. It does in fact identify – whether wittingly or unwittingly – the germ of an important truth, reminding us that the internet is merely a system for communicating data. It is powerful in terms of its speed and capacity, but conceptually no different from any other communications system. Moreover, the internet is dependent on the effectiveness of another communications system, that of the telephone. Data is actually transmitted along the same wires and microwave links as voice signals. It is precisely for that reason that it has been possible for its use to spread so rapidly in those countries where there has been virtually universal access to voice telecommunications for several decades. Considered simply as a communication system, the internet is not conceptually new.

Why then is it argued to be so different? The difference lies not in the fact of providing a global communications system, but rather in how the system works. The internet is essentially a tool for using communications systems rather than being a system in its own right. The various technologies that make it work were designed for this purpose. The internet is best understood not as an end in itself, but as a means to an end – the communication of information. Physical communications provide an apt analogy: the importance of a car lies not in its external appearance nor even in the size of its engine, but in its ability to perform the task of transporting its driver and passengers from A to B. In the jargon of management, we judge it by its fitness for purpose. Similarly, the social, economic and political significance of the internet lies not in the technologies that make it work, but in the fact that it facilitates communication.

The real difference between the internet and previous systems of communication lies in what is being transmitted and the relationship between the source and the receiver. The telephone is a mechanism that allows two people to speak to each other regardless of where they are physically located, provided they do so synchronously. The original electric telegraph, and wireless telegraphy that followed it, were designed to transmit electrical impulses which the receiver could interpret to reconstruct the original message. Telephony and telegraphy both take place in real time, because the source and the receiver must be simultaneously connected to the system. The internet is different because of the technology that links the receiver and the source.

The internet links computers. That simple statement of the obvious is the key to understanding what is fundamentally new about it. Computers store as well as process information, and the systems that support the internet are built around this fact. Consider the simplified form of the Shannon and Weaver model in Figure 3.1.

This does not, however, fully describe the way in which the internet works in practice. Figure 3.2 uses a similar method of representation.

This adaptation of the Shannon and Weaver model illustrates how the internet overcomes the tyranny of time. This is perhaps most easily explained by considering how an e-mail message is transmitted, as shown in Figure 3.3.

This illustrates the fact that the sender and the recipient of the e-mail need not be simultaneously connected to the communications system, because the system incorporates a storage mechanism to which the message is initially transmitted. The recipient has access to this store, and can therefore retrieve the message at any time. It is this that makes the internet unique as a system of communication: it allows asynchronous use of a telecommunications system. It does this because it links not telephones, or telegraphic equipment, but computers.

The internet and the world wide web

At the heart of the internet are the computers that mediate between the source and the receiver. In Figure 3.3, we used the example of an

SOURCE ➤ TRANSMITTER ➤ RECEIVER

Fig. 3.1 *The Shannon and Weaver model*

SOURCE ➤ TRANSMITTER ➤ STORE ➤ TRANSMITTER ➤ RECEIVER

Fig. 3.2 *The Shannon and Weaver model adapted to the internet*

Message keyed by sender	SOURCE
Message sent to store	TRANSMITTER
Message stored	STORE
Message retrieved by recipient	TRANSMITTER
Message received	RECEIVER

Fig. 3.3 *Sending and receiving an e-mail*

e-mail to explain this, but the same model can be adapted to illustrate the essentials of the operation of the world wide web. A website is held on a host computer; it is that computer that is accessed by the user who seeks access to the site, and the internet provides the communications links from the machine that hosts the site to the machine being used by the searcher. In Figure 3.4, we show how this works.

To achieve the communication represented in Figure 3.4, three conditions must be met:

- It must be possible to identify a particular site.
- The searcher must know how to access that site.
- The site must be accessible.

The URL

The world wide web meets all of these conditions. The identification of sites is achieved by the system of the Uniform Resource Locator,

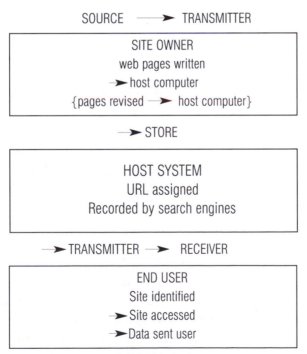

Fig. 3.4 *Communicating on the world wide web*

or URL, which in turn is derived from the internationally recognized system for creating e-mail addresses. The URL is the web equivalent of a reference to a printed source such as those we are using in our notes. The conventions are widely understood, and enable us to provide unambiguous references from which the reader can, at will, trace the work to which we are referring. A URL has exactly the same function; when we quote that, the reader with access to the web can go directly to the site that we have indicated.

The elements of the URL are the names of the site, the domain in which it is located, and its country of origin. We can illustrate this with some simple examples:

* pro.gov.uk
* bbc.co.uk
* ox.ac.uk

These are, respectively, the web addresses of the Public Record Office, the British Broadcasting Corporation and the University of Oxford. The most important element of the URL is the first part, and this is typically (as in these cases) a familiar acronym, an obvious abbreviation, or sometimes a mnemonic. The two remaining elements of the URL are the domain name and the country indicator. The domain indicates what sort of organization is providing the site; thus, in the UK we have such domains as **.ac** (for universities and colleges), **.gov** (for central and local government), and **.co** (for commercial enterprises). Other countries differ slightly; in the USA, for example, the equivalent of the British **.ac** is **.edu**. The country indicator is used only when the site owner is not in the USA, or in cases where the more prestigious (and more expensive) **.com** is used instead of **.co**.

Finally, the URL also contains some technical information, including the system used for encoding the data (normally http, or Hypertext Transfer Protocol) and the fact that it refers to a website (www) as opposed to some other system. Thus the full version of the Public Record Office's URL is **http://www.pro.gov.uk**.

The URL meets the first condition for communicating on the web. The second is met by the various search engines that allow the user to find the site which is being sought. Search engines are the web equivalent of a whole range of traditional printed reference books, such as directories, indexes and bibliographies. They are, however, far more powerful, because they use the capacity of computers to search vast amounts of data at great speed. The search can be very specific, or very general. If the name of an organization is known, using a search engine is like using a phone book; the name is entered and the URL of the organization will be shown. But, unlike conventional reference sources, we can also use a search engine to conduct a more generalized search. Almost any term can be used; no particular skills are required to undertake the search. The search engine will produce a list of websites, with a couple of lines of information about each, and a URL which can be accessed immediately by a click of the mouse because of the hypermedia basis of the web.

The major public access search engines, such as Yahoo!, AltaVista, Lycos, HotBot and so on, are commercial enterprises, which are able to provide a free service to users because they sell advertising space. They continuously monitor the web for new sites and index them appropriately. Yahoo!, for example, has a long list of 'categories', which are effectively a sub-division of its indexing system. Thus a search on Yahoo! for a particular term will yield **n** categories and **x** sites. This takes less time to do than it takes to read this description of it. The search engines are, for the user, the motive power of the web.[3]

Accessibility

The final condition is that of accessibility. In the terminology of the Shannon and Weaver model, the source must be accessible, and the receiver must have access. This is achieved rather differently at each end of the communication chain, and is dependent on the intermediate store illustrated in Figure 3.4. The site itself – the source – is typically always online. The data is held on a disk in a dedicated computer – known as a server – which is permanently connected to the internet. This can, in theory, be any PC, and any telephone line capable of carrying digital data can be used. In practice, it is only large organizations such as universities or major companies that maintain their own servers on a so-called 7/24 basis.[4] Smaller organizations and the millions of individuals who have their own sites use Internet

Service Providers (ISPs) such as Hotmail, Geocities and so on. The file space for the site is, once again, often provided free to the site owner; the ISP makes a profit out of advertising revenues and from other activities.

The ISPs do not only provide a hosting service for websites. They also provide access to users at the other end of the communication chain. The major ISPs such as MSN, AOL and CompuServe are among the giants of the global information industry.[5] It is through them that any PC can be linked to the internet, as illustrated in Figure 3.5.

The ISP is the link between the server and the telecommunications system, and between that system and the end user. The user subscribes to an ISP, through which any site on the web can be accessed. A typical search is illustrated in Figure 3.6.

This model is generally applicable regardless of the ISPs involved. Although most ISPs are commercial enterprises, some are provided at public expense. In the UK, for example, the Joint Academic NETwork (JANET) is provided to all higher education institutions for uncharged use by their staff and students. But it can be used to search the whole web, regardless of the status of the ISP of the site owner, and can itself be searched using any ISP and search engine.[6] Other public networks include those provided by governments in many countries. The ISPs that link servers to the telecommunications net-

SERVER → ISP → TELECOMMS NETWORK → ISP → END USER

Fig. 3.5   *The ISP in the communication chain*

SUBSCRIBER → ISP → SEARCH ENGINE
{SEARCH PERFORMED BY SEARCH ENGINE}
{SITE SELECTED BY SUBSCRIBER}
 → TELECOMMS NETWORK → ISP → SERVER
 → ISP → TELECOMMS NETWORK → ISP → SUBSCRIBER

Fig. 3.6   *Finding and accessing a website*

works and end-users to those same networks are, therefore, the critical final link in the chain of accessibility from source to receiver.

Most of what has been described in this section became commonplace in the last five years of the 20th century. Until the mid-1990s, the internet was still the esoteric preserve of academics and computer enthusiasts.[7] The change happened at a pace that was more revolutionary than evolutionary, and can be traced through various guides that were published at the time. In 1992, the American publisher Addison-Wesley published what was claimed to be the 'first computer trade book to introduce the world to the wonders of the Internet'. This book, *The internet companion: a beginner's guide to global networking* by Tracy Laquey, had a preface by the newly elected Vice-President of the USA, Al Gore, in which he proclaimed the new administration's commitment to the development of the information superhighway.[8] There was a similar sense of pioneering and even evangelism about other books published at the time; they assume that the reader is unfamiliar with the internet and the newly launched web.[9] Yet by 1995, a book aimed specifically at the British market (which was probably a few months behind developments in the USA) could simply assume the reader's familiarity with the web. Although it still asked 'Why use the internet?', the question was half-hearted.[10] When *The internet and the world wide web: the rough guide* asked in its 1998 edition 'So is the net still basically a geek hangout?', the question was frivolous, and the answer was 'no'.[11] The establishment of the internet, and particularly the web and e-mail, as part of the daily life of hundreds of millions of people across the globe is perhaps the most potent of all illustrations of the impact of technological change on the communication of information.

The dilemma of quality

It is of the very essence of the internet that it is open to all. It is the most public space that has ever been created, for it is participative and interactive not merely a passive conveyor of information. Habermas argued that the mass media had degraded the traditional public space within which discourse and debate had taken place. Others followed his line of thought (perhaps further than he would go himself) to argue that the mass media – and particularly television – were working to the lowest common denominator of public taste and ignoring all but the most popular activities and the most anodyne views. Even the development of cable and satellite broadcasting merely served to proliferate the number of channels showing worthless programmes, to which the few exceptions prove the rule.[12] In practice, of course, the mass media are not a public space at all in Habermas's sense, for television – the medium that this argument is really about – is a one-way street from source to receiver. The internet clearly is not.

Anyone can participate in the public space of the internet. In Figure 3.5, we illustrated how the ISP plays a critical part in facilitating communication between source and receiver on the internet. In Figure 3.6, we schematized a search of the world wide web. In both cases, we argued for the validity of the Shannon and Weaver model, just as it has been validly applied to other means of communication from telegraphy to broadcasting. Let us, however, consider two specific applications of the model. In modelling a telephone system (which was Shannon's prime concern), Shannon and Weaver were, of course, assuming two-way communication. The 'source' was the person making the call or conveying the information, but the communication was interactive and, indeed, as we have seen, synchronous. Either party could initiate the call and influence its content. The same is manifestly not true of broadcasting, where the source – the broadcaster – determines the timing, content and availability of the communication. The receiver is simply the passive recipient, and even the development of cheap and simple video recording systems, which allow the recipient to vary the time at which the broadcast is actually watched, does not have any significant impact on this model. Even digital broadcasting systems that give the viewer some (but very limited) control over what is shown on the screen do not materially change the position.[13]

In this respect, the internet combines features of both the interactive, but synchronous, communication of the telephone call and the passive, but potentially asynchronous, broadcast recorded by the receiver. Any user of the internet can access more or less everything that is there, just as the subscriber to satellite television can watch any channel; but equally any user can provide material and make it available to all other users, just as anyone with a telephone can initiate a call and determine its content. The web has made it possible for anyone to be a publisher of information, virtually without limitation on content or subject matter, and with no control on the quality of the information that is provided. Whether this is electronic democracy or electronic anarchy, it is certainly an electronic public space.

Lack of government control

The issues that this raises are central to the workings of the information society. Governments have lost control – probably irretrievably – of much over which they previously exercised their authority. The most obvious area, in the sense that it probably causes most concern, is that of the moral censorship of sexual material. This has always been a particularly difficult aspect of what is now called information policy, depending as it does on religious beliefs, social norms and personal taste and opinion. It is a field into which politicians and judges venture not without encountering serious difficulties, but at least in the age of print and broadcasting some control could be exercised if it was thought desirable.[14] Pornographic magazines were indeed available, either legally or illegally, in most western countries, and satellite broadcasting brought semi-pornographic television to countries in which it could be broadcast. The web brought it into the home. The response of the ISPs was to give the subscriber a mechanism for controlling access to websites, and then classifying sites in much the same way that movies have been always been classified for public exhibition in the cinema or on television. At least one of the search engines (Yahoo!) exercises its right to exclude certain websites from its indexes on moral grounds.[15] But it takes no great ingenuity to circumvent the system, especially at a time when many children are still more adept than their parents at using computers and surfing the web. Legal prohibitions on certain kinds of material, enforced for centuries on printers and publishers, and for decades on movie makers and broadcasters, have all but vanished in less than ten years.

The social and political implications go far beyond the murky area of moral censorship. Because it is so easy and so cheap to create a website and make it accessible to all, it is no longer possible for governments or indeed media organizations to control the dissemination of news or so easy for them to influence the development of public opinion.

An example will illustrate the point. In the summer of 2000, a former employee of the British security service, MI5, was under arrest on charges under the Official Secrets Act, having returned voluntarily to Britain from a period of self-imposed exile in France.[16] David Shayler had made a series of accusations against MI5, including that of engaging in an illegal conspiracy to assassinate President Gaddafy of Libya. The bulk of his material was published on his own website, including details which no British newspaper would have dared to publish nor any British network to broadcast.[17] A search in August 2000 revealed some 1600 web pages that refer to Shayler,[18] although his own website was no longer accessible. For all practical purposes, despite the inaccessibility of Shayler's own site, the whole story, including (especially) the parts the UK government would prefer to suppress, was in the public domain. The fact that Shayler's accusation is known does not, however, tell us anything about its truth. It can be cogently argued that the web has made it more difficult for governments and other powerful organizations to suppress information that they would prefer was not released, and less easy for them to distort information that is in the public domain. On the other hand, there are none of the traditional controls over the quality of the information that we find in other public communications systems. Quality control of the information on websites lies entirely in the hands of the site owners, who may verify as much or as little as they wish. Although it is now generally accepted that it is possible to defame a person on a website (or indeed in an e-mail), and to seek redress through the courts, there is no system that can guarantee that information is accurate even when it is not defamatory of an individual or an organization.[19]

Lack of quality control

The contrast with traditional systems is marked. One of the key roles of print publishers, whether of books, newspapers or magazines, has been to exercise a degree of control over the quality of what is published in their name. This is, of course, understood in different ways by different publishers. A book that is acceptable to one publisher or editor may not be acceptable to another; standards vary from the impeccable to the invisible. But the controls are there. Moreover, the sheer cost of traditional publishing of print on paper deters all but the most determined of those who cannot find a publisher to issue their work. No such quality controls, and no such financial deterrents, exist on the web. Ironically, it is in the multiplicity of printed guides to the use of the internet, and particularly of the web, that we find the best evaluation of websites,[20] although some ISPs and search engines do offer selective or even evaluative listings.[21] Essentially, however, the asessment of quality lies with the user, and its control with the provider. This should not, however, lead us to assume, as some writers do, that there is no quality control; many providers are assiduous and offer material of great depth and quality.[22] There are good and bad websites just as there are good and bad books and journals; quality is dependent on effective writing and editing, not on the medium of transmission.

Nevertheless, the web does significantly modify a familiar communication paradigm, which is also ultimately derived from the Shannon and Weaver model.

In Figure 3.7, we give a very simplified version of a conventional representation of print-on-paper publishing as a communication system. Moreover, this applies to many other conventional systems for the storage and dissemination of information, including audio and video recordings, and indeed computer software. At the heart of it is the publisher, an all-inclusive term that we use to mean the person or company responsible for the selection, production and distribution of information in a material form. This form might be a book, a newspaper, a periodical, a videotape, an audio CD, or a floppy disk; the principle remains the same.

The dissemination of information through a website is manifestly different in more than the technology that is used. In terms of Figure 3.7, the publisher is eliminated from the process. Indeed, the web

Fig. 3.7 *From author to reader*

Fig. 3.8   *From author to reader on the web*

equivalent starkly illustrates the directness of the web (Figure 3.8).
Of course, all the technical components of the Shannon and Weaver
model are still present, but we have omitted them here, just as we
have in Figure 3.7. This is because we are now looking at communication in a slightly different sense. We are no longer focusing on the
technical mechanisms of transmitting data from A to B, but at the
content of the data that is transmitted. In effect, a website is a direct
mechanism for authors to communicate with readers, to use the
terms of conventional publishing. In terms of another medium, we
might argue that this is broadcasting (that is communication from
one to many) under the control of an individual.[23] This last analogy,
which is a strong one, perhaps serves to emphasize the significance of
what the web has facilitated. Whereas once broadcasting was the preserve of vast and powerful corporations, often operating with monopoly franchises and sometimes under state control, it is now open,
through a slightly different medium, to everyone with internet
access.[24]

The implications of changes in the technology of communications
are very significant. We do not need to be technological determinists
to accept that the invention of printing was at least a partial cause of
a fundamental transformation of intellectual, economic and political
life in western Europe. The same is true of the development of com-
puter-based information and communications technologies in the second half of the 20th century. The power of computers to store,
handle and retrieve information, and the capacity of telecommunications systems to transmit it instantaneously and globally, represents a
real break with the past. Whether or not that break is conceptual is
still a matter for debate; but there can be no doubt of its practical
implications. We have already touched on some of these, such as the
availability of material on the web.

We now turn to a more systematic study of how society is coping
with these changes. At a societal level, this is necessarily takes us into
the political arena. The regulation of telecommunications and broad-

casting networks, for example, is a matter for governments and international bodies. So too is any moral or political control over the content of media, whether printed, broadcast or digital. The law regulates the ownership of content, and of data. Political considerations determine the accessibility of information. Governments, however, are only one group of stakeholders; even if we reject the extremes of the Machlup–Porat theory of the knowledge-based society, it is clear that no country can ignore both the negative and the positive implications of changes in information and communications technologies. In Chapter 4, we shall examine the general principles of the role of the state and other bodies in this area, and the basic principles of what is generally called *information policy*. In Chapter 5, we shall examine more closely how some countries and groups of countries are addressing the issues in practice, to lever for themselves the perceived benefits of the information society.

A note on further reading

Much of the material covered by this chapter is still ill-served by formal literature. The best way to learn about the web is to use it. The student who makes intelligent use of search engines and printed guides, and applies an understanding of the principles that underlie the web, will learn a great deal about how information is most effectively organized and retrieved. The impact of the web on other forms of communication is still inevitably a matter of speculation and disagreement. Herman and McChesney (note 24) are to some extent sceptical, and their work is now a few years old (significant in this field), but it is still essential reading.

Notes and references

1   See above, pp. 7–9.
2   T. Standage, *The Victorian internet: the remarkable story of the telegraph and the 19th century's online pioneers*, Weidenfeld and Nicolson, 1998.
3   For an evaluative list of search engines, see
    http://www.searchenginewatch.com.

 4 7/24 is the current UK jargon for operating 7 days a week and
    24 hours a day.
 5 The ISPs are listed in most guides to the web; as an example,
    see the current (2000) edition of *The internet and the world wide
    web: the rough guide*, Rough Guides Ltd, 2000, and the company's
    website at
    http://www.roughguides.com
 6 We should emphasize that the statement about the use of
    JANET in this sentence is *technical*. There are regulatory limita-
    tions on how it can be used in practice.
 7 We use a polite word! Others were more common at the time.
 8 The quotation is from the preface to the second edition pub-
    lished in 1994.
 9 The many examples include Elizabeth Lane Lawley and Craig
    Summerhill, *Internet primer for information professionals*, Meckler-
    media, 1993 and Gilster, P., *The internet navigator*, John Wiley
    and Sons, 1993.
10 Ivan Pope, *Internet UK*, Prentice Hall, 1995. The quotations are
    on p. 1 and p. 3 respectively.
11 *The internet and the world wide web: the rough guide*, Rough Guides
    Ltd, 3rd edn, 1998, 17.
12 Without necessarily endorsing this line of argument, we note
    that of the more than 100 channels available in the UK through
    the Sky digital satellite television service, BSB (owned by News
    Corporation), only a handful carry anything other than sport,
    light entertainment or popular movies.
13 We are referring to such systems as that used on the Sky Inter-
    active Sports channel in the UK, where the viewer can select
    from four camera angles, follow a particular player (selected by
    the broadcaster) round the field, or look at statistical data,
    replays of key incidents in the game, and so on. But control
    remains with the broadcaster. There is no genuine interactivity
    because the viewer can only take what the broadcaster offers; he
    or she cannot select the player to follow, for example, nor move
    the cameras.
14 See below, pp. 67–9. We deal in detail with information policy
    issues in Chapter 4.
15 See below, p. 62 and note 10 in Chapter 4, for a particular case

involving Yahoo!

16 All the British newspapers carried the story in the week of 21 August 2000.

17 Although Shayler's original allegations did appear in the British press, at least in part. They first surfaced in the *Mail on Sunday*, a right wing tabloid, on 24 August 1997. But the flood of injunctions soon began to flow.

18 Search conducted on Yahoo! on 23 August 2000.

19 For a discussion of quality issues, see Gordon Graham, *The internet: a philosophical inquiry*, Routledge, 1999, 89–93.

20 Such as that in note 5, above.

21 Both AOL and MSN, for example, have links from their home pages to selected categories of sites on such subjects as recreation, news and entertainment; it is not clear how or by whom they are selected. Similarly Yahoo! offers a service that identifies '101 most useful sites', but this is a printed magazine available only on subscription (see **http://www.zdnet.com/zdsubs/yahoo/tree/ yen.html**).

22 Everard, 127–32.

23 We are not here referring to webcasting, the use of the multimedia capacity of the web to transmit programmes that are also broadcast by radio and television. We are simply using a metaphor to draw an analogy and define a contrast.

24 This point is denied by Edward S. Herman and Robert W. McChesney, *The global media: the new missionaries of global capitalism*, Cassell, 1997, 196. But even these authors (who consistently downplay the impact of the internet on communications and the mass media) admit that it easier to set up a website than to start a cable television channel (p. 191). In fairness to these distinguished scholars, it should be added that they were writing in 1996–7 when the potential impact of the web was still difficult to assess.

4

Information policy

Using information in the information society

The information society foretold, described and analysed by the theorists has become identified, in the public mind, with the digital technologies that support data storage and processing. The perception is that these technologies are the cause of fundamental changes in the ways in which people live and work. Even for the technological determinists, however, such a statement is too crude. The direct impact of technological change is largely confined to those in the industrialized countries, and within them to an educated and wealthy minority. The minority is growing; over half the population of the UK has a mobile phone, and one-third have access to the internet. Numbers of users of both are growing daily. In many countries, however, growth is slower, and in some parts of the world, whether for political or economic reasons, or both, developments are so slow as to be almost imperceptible. Even the most basic networks for voice telecommunications are rarely wholly reliable in some parts of Latin America, eastern Europe, Asia and Africa.[1]

The contrasts are stark indeed when we look at the statistical data. In 1996, it was estimated that only 20% of the world's population has ever initiated a telephone call.[2] The context for this is to be found in the fact that three years later, in 1999, the 12% of the world's population who lived in Africa had only 2% of the telephone lines.[3] This imbalance has, of course, a direct impact on internet usage. In 1997, 73% of all users of the world wide web were in the USA, and only 4% in *all* the developing countries together.[4] In 1999, of the 158 million people around the world with internet access, 125.1 million were in the industrialized countries. Of the remainder, 26 million were in south-east Asia, and just over 1 million in sub-Saharan Africa.[5] Among the latter, 700,000 were in comparatively well-developed South Africa.[6]

One important lesson to be learned from this is that networked computing has not displaced all previous information systems. Just as handwriting survived the invention of printing, so handwriting, printing and voice communications will survive into the age of the computer. Nevertheless, it is undeniable that there has been great change. Certain kinds of information are now more commonly available electronically than on paper, and much more is accessible in both forms. And it is the applications of computing, and particularly the mushroom growth of the internet, which has made the information society a subject of such widespread public interest and concern. The internet is not confined by the traditional boundaries of the nations, races or classes. It is international, universal and, for those who, choose, anonymous. It allows virtually instantaneous global communication of data of all kinds, and for that reason underpins the phenomenon of globalization.

The global information society

Globalization – a word that has entered both common and academic usage only since the late 1980s[7] – is closely associated with development of the knowledge-based economy of the information society. Castells argues that the 'informational economy' (as he usually calls it) is indeed the principal driver of globalization.[8] What this means in practice is that competition and production have become global. Indeed, it was in manufacturing industry that globalization first began.[9] In the comparatively simple area of the manufacture of goods, this is obvious. East Asian motor car companies make their cars in factories in Europe; indeed European governments vie with each other for the privilege of hosting the factories. Products travel around the world, so that the supermarkets of Europe and North America are stocked with produce from Africa, Asia and Australasia as well as their own continents year-round. The invisible economy – the economy of the money markets, the stock exchanges, insurance and financial services – is not merely global but continuous, working every hour of every day throughout the year. To a greater or lesser extent, all of this is dependent on the exchange of information and the existence of a network infrastructure to facilitate it.

Globalization, however, is more than merely economic. It has vast political consequences. It can be cogently argued to have undermined the sovereignty of the nation states that have dominated world history for the last 400 years. The beneficiaries are the major corporations that control almost every aspect of the global economy. While they are subject to the governments of the territories in which they operate, they can nevertheless exert great influence over those governments both overtly and covertly, while traditional legal systems are sometimes rendered impotent to control them. In a well-publicized case, a French judge has admitted that he could see no technical mechanisms by which the Yahoo! search engine could be prevented from allowing users in France (but not in other countries) to access websites that were illegal in that country.[10] Satellite broadcasting systems are increasingly subject to international or European Union law, rather than national legislation, custom and practice.[11] The threat to withdraw a production facility can force a change of policy; a media tycoon who rules a global empire can determine editorial policies across the globe to influence electorates; operators in the money markets can sustain or ruin entire economies. Such companies and individuals can move easily from a country where the law is unfavourable to them to one where it is not; or they can influence changes in law and policy for their benefit.[12] The beneficiary countries and organizations are able to inhibit and sometimes to prevent the development of global regulatory regimes that would make such movements of capital impossible and hence reduce the influence of the global corporations. Nor is globalization confined to legitimate activities. Criminals, especially in such lucrative areas as illicit drugs and money laundering, are also beneficiaries of easy global communications and weak international jurisdictions.[13] In different ways, and with varying degrees of concern and disapproval, all commentators are agreed that global systems of communication (physical as well as virtual) make this possible, and have perhaps made it inevitable.[14]

The underlying assumption of a symbiosis between knowledge and power is perhaps the most common theme of this aspect of the analysis of the information society. Access to information through communications systems is therefore the key to the acquisition and sustenance of power. The converse is also true, and is a major political issue throughout the world. The trend towards the knowledge economy in Europe and North America, which, as we have seen, has been observed and discussed for almost half a century, has destroyed many traditional occupations. Whole industries have vanished, or been decimated. Shipbuilding, steel production, coal mining, textiles, even agriculture, which were once the powerhouses of the advanced economies, have now moved to other countries or been superseded altogether. Whole groups in society have been the victims of the change in the market for their carefully honed traditional skills, and have found themselves without the means to acquire the new skills that are in demand. By and large, despite the exhortations of politicians, people cannot move to jobs, especially if those jobs are in other countries that themselves have surplus labour. The result has been a profound change in the patterns of work in the west with more part-time working, more home-based working, more female employment, less security of tenure. What Castells calls the 'transformation of work' is, for millions of people across the globe, the most personal impact that the post-industrial or information society has had on their lives.[15]

The problem of the decline of traditional industrial jobs is compounded by the lack of mechanisms for the reskilling of the workforce. Indeed, western Europe is now so short of the skills needed for the development and exploitation of the new technologies that there is serious talk of importing skilled labour from elsewhere in the world.[16] To some extent, this is a reaction to the *de facto* export of jobs. Data input and processing can easily be outsourced to companies that operate in cheap labour markets such as India, Thailand or the Philippines, where a large and pliant labour force can be supported by a technological and professional infrastructure which is adequate for the purpose. Increasingly, western governments are recognizing that policies need to be developed that will enable communication and information technologies to make a positive contribution to the change in labour market, and to alleviate the social exclusion that they have partly created.[17] More generally, these governments are acknowledging their obligation to deal with the issues that arise out of the development of the information society, at many levels and in many different aspects of policy. Information policy is no longer confined to a few narrow traditional areas, but is reaching out into all those many aspects of society in which information itself is now a major player.

Information policy: an introduction

There is, observe two astute commentators, 'no consensus about what constitutes information policy.'[18] The problem is that the potential scope of such a policy is so broad, and is becoming broader as information becomes more generally recognized as an overt element in so many aspects of political, economic and social life. Information policy has a long history, far longer than the use of the phrase itself. Historically, it encompasses such matters as copyright, data protection, freedom of the press and freedom of information.[19] All of these are activities in which states have involved themselves for many centuries. It is no longer possible, however, to draw a hard and fast line between these traditional areas of information policy, and policies that facilitate access to information and its effective use. Such areas include, for example, the regulation of telecommunications networks and broadcasting systems, in terms of technological infrastructures, ownership, access and use; the alleviation of the consequences of information poverty through education, social provision and training; the provision of libraries and other public access information services and institutions; and the provision of information to citizens. Unlike most traditional information policies, much of this domain is politically controversial and has very significant financial implications for social welfare, education and other aspects of public investment and expenditure.[20]

We shall deal first with the traditional core areas of information policy, before considering some of the wider implications.

Freedom of the press
Print media

Freedom of the press – the right to publish without ideological control – has been a live issue for at least 350 years. Pre-publication censorship developed in the wake of the invention of printing. From the middle of the 15th century to the middle of the 17th, it was normal in western Europe for secular and ecclesiastical authorities to control the output of the press. There was, of course, some surreptitious printing, but when discovered it was punished, often harshly. Gradually controls were relaxed, or were no longer enforceable. In the United Provinces (the modern Netherlands), a state that was developed in the late 16th century out of a rebellion against Spanish rule, the press was free in all but name by the middle of the 17th century. Some, although by no means all, of the cantons that formed the Swiss Confederation (modern Switzerland) had similarly light controls. In the middle of the 17th century, the English republican poet John Milton made the case for a free press.[21] He could only do so because he was living in the midst of a revolution in the course of which a rigid system of censorship had collapsed. His plea, eloquent as it was, went largely unheard, and the republican government of which he was a part imposed controls as strict as those of the monarchy that it had overthrown. In the longer term, however, Milton was to have significant influence both in his own country and in 18th-century America. Eventually, pre-publication censorship in England came to an end in 1693, although stringent penalties remained against those who published politically or religiously unacceptable works.[22]

It was not until the end of the 18th century that formal censorship began to vanish elsewhere. In 1790, the First Amendment to the new American constitution guaranteed (as it still does) freedom of the press.[23] Various French revolutionary constitutions offered similar guarantees, and during the 19th century a free press came to be seen as one of the hallmarks of a liberal democratic state. By the end of the 20th century, freedom of the press was incorporated into such documents as the Universal Declaration of Human Rights sponsored by the United Nations, although the extent to which countries adhered to its provisions was, at best, variable. The collapse of European communism in 1989–90 brought with it a new freedom to publish in eastern Europe, in Russia and in some of the other successor states of the former Soviet Union. It was not, however, universal. In many countries in Africa and Asia the press is still subject to controls, which take many forms. These include state ownership of some or all newspapers (common in many sub-Saharan African countries); formal censorship before publication or distribution (in Saudi Arabia, for example); subsequent punishment for the infringement of strict laws (Pakistan and elsewhere); self-censorship by editors who know the limits and abide by them even though there is no written code;[24] or privileged access to information, which makes a particular newspaper at least the semi-official voice of government (*Al Ahram* in Egypt being a widely quoted example).

Moreover, the right to publish is rarely, if ever, absolute. Even in the USA, which probably – in this sense – has the most free press in the world, there are limitations imposed by laws relating to defamation, pornography and similar protection for individuals and prohibitions on certain classes of publication. In Britain the notorious device of the injunction allows individuals, companies and the government to prevent the publication of material that they prefer not to see in print. In recent years, however, the courts have become somewhat less sympathetic to this use of injunctions, especially in political cases. The injunction is a tool for the rich and the powerful, and certainly does nothing to sharpen the incisiveness of the British press. In the democratic countries, however, the ownership of the media is probably a greater inhibition on the freedom to publish than is formal legal constraint.[25]

Broadcast media

Although freedom of the press developed, historically, in the context of print, similar regimes surround the broadcast media. In most countries, the state has a significant role in broadcasting. In many countries in Africa and Asia, the state is the monopoly broadcaster, as it was in eastern Europe and in the former Soviet Union. In western Europe, and in the post-communist states of the east, state ownership of at least part of the television and radio broadcasting network is normal, even if control is at arm's length as in the British model. Even in the USA, the Federal Communications Commission issues licences to broadcast nationally and regionally, although the producers and networks are private companies.[26] Broadcasters themselves are ultra-cautious, especially on moral issues. The British '9 o'clock watershed' is what many would no doubt regard as a typical British compromise, allowing so-called 'adult' material to be broadcast after that time.[27] Other countries are less concerned about such matters; there are Dutch and Scandinavian channels that regularly broadcast pornography some of which can be seen in Britain by satellite and cable subscribers, although subject to certain controls including a law that permits the Home Secretary to ban named channels.[28] By contrast, much British comedy material is wholly unacceptable to the mainstream networks in the USA, because of the situations portrayed and the language used.

As with the print media, much of the censorship in television is self-imposed by the broadcasters themselves. The same has always been partly true of the cinema. In the most important producer country, the USA, a self-regulatory moral code (the Hays Code) was introduced in 1930, following the rapid development of the talkies and a number of Hollywood scandals, most notably the rape allegations against the comic actor Fatty Arbuckle.[29] The Hays Code ensured that American (and hence much world) cinema purveyed a middle class, Christian, moral message for decades.[30] In Britain, the British Board of Film Censors, founded by the film industry itself in 1912, issued certificates without which a movie would not normally be shown publicly. Each movie was graded as U (for general exhibition) or A (for adults only). This scheme was modified over the years to allow children over a certain age to see A-rated films under certain circumstances, and by introducing the X classification for adults only. Its successor body, the statutory British Board of Film Classification, despite the more anodyne language of its title, has done much the same thing since its establishment in 1985.[31] Television channels use the certification of movies to determine their own practices, although the satellite and cable movie channels have developed their own systems and indeed in some cases an earlier 'watershed'. The censorship of the cinema, both at the time of production and at the time of exhibition, is accepted in most democratic countries in a way in which press censorship is not. It seems that pictures are thought to be more dangerous than words.

Censorship

The development of the internet, and particularly of the multimedia capacity of the web, has raised a host of new issues about censorship. Even in pre-web days, the **.alt** and **.sex** sites were among the most frequently visited. Now, hard-core pornography, of a kind that would be banned from public sale in printed form in all but a handful of north-west European countries, is easily available. The fact that it is normally charged for (via a credit card) is probably only a minor deterrent. Some internet service providers do put limits on what they will permit on websites that they host, as some search engines do on the sites they will index. Governments, however, have proved inept and impotent in regulating the content of the internet, even when they have wished to do so. In the USA, the Communications Decency Act of 1995 put the onus of responsibility for website content on the ISPs and made them liable for prosecution if they infringed its provisions. The Supreme Court struck down the Act as being unconstitutional by restricting First Amendment rights to free speech.[32] Australian attempts to replicate the patterns of film classification are at best partially successful, and advisory.[33] The only developed state that has succeeded in making a significant impact on the problem – if it is a problem – is Singapore. The three ISPs that are allowed to function there are regulated by the notoriously strict Singapore Broadcasting Authority. In the neighbouring state of Malaysia, by contrast and despite the drive towards islamicization, there has been a decision in principle not to censor the web, partly because it is impractical and partly because there is a perception of a competitive edge over Singapore.[34]

In practice, and with the sole exception of the tightly regulated city state of Singapore, the only real means of preventing access in countries with advanced telecommunications systems lies in the hands of the individual user. Account holders who subscribe to an ISP can impose limits on what can be accessed through particular passwords, which they control, thus preventing their children from accessing sites deemed to be 'unsuitable'. The suitability is determined by the individual site owners and to a limited extent the ISPs and search engine providers, who have, in effect, reinvented the self-censorship of the broadcasters and the movie makers for this purpose.

Freedom of the press and censorship are the most philosophically complex area of information policy. Press freedom is a cherished democratic right, yet few would advocate the complete abolition of all control over any the media. Even among the notoriously free spirits of the internet, there is a broad acceptance of the need for some

controls if only to protect the young. It is an arena in which governments trespass at their peril. By and large, public policy is designed
to protect the vulnerable in general terms, and the courts are left to
take the opprobrium of such enforcement as is possible.

Copyright

Copyright also has its origins in the concern about controlling the
press in early modern Europe, but it has taken a very different subsequent path. It originated from the need to maintain registers of
publications and publishers, but has been transformed into a right
that protects authors against the improper or unapproved use of
their work.[35] Moreover, during the 19th century, copyright and
related laws were extended to cover such productions as pictures,
sculptures, designs and musical compositions. More recently, it has
come to encompass recorded sound, broadcasts, movies and computer software. It even includes the unrecorded spoken word and
public events. The law relating to copyright and what the lawyers call
'adjacent' rights is now only one part of the law of intellectual property, which also includes such matters as patents for inventions and
other protections for the products of the human intellect.[36]

The essence of modern copyright law is that authors, or other creators,[37] have complete control over their reproducible or performable
creations, although in practice the creator's rights are typically sold
or licensed to others to facilitate commercial exploitation. This goes
far beyond the most obvious cases such as a book or other written
work. It is because of this principle that the promoters of sporting
events can sell the right to broadcast or record the event. Such rights
have become a vital source of income to most sports, especially those
that have international appeal such as soccer or the Olympic Games.
An important dimension of this is the concept of the author's 'moral
right' to control how the material is used, to enable objections to be
raised, for example, to the use of a copyright photograph or a piece
of music in an advertisement for a product of which the copyright
owner disapproves.

Since the late 19th century, copyright has been internationalized.
The Berne Convention of 1886 gave full reciprocal protection to the
citizens of all signatory states. Virtually every country in the world is

now a signatory both of this and of the similar Universal Copyright Convention, developed by UNESCO in 1956. Moreover, international copyright law is, broadly speaking, enforced. It is in the interests of authors and publishers to do so. It provides an orderly global legislative framework, within which the information industry can function, although it is currently under severe strain because of the near impossibility of policing the use of material on the internet.[38]

Copyright law has two aspects, which partly conflict with each other. This is sometimes presented as a contrast between different systems of laws, particularly English and French. It is argued that in the English common law tradition, inherited by much of the world including the USA, it is the commercial rights of the copyright owner that are the centre of attention. By contrast, the argument goes, in the French system, derived from the *Code Napoléon* and widely imitated in continental Europe, the law is primarily there to protect the *droit moral* – the moral right – of the creator, while recognizing a general interest by the whole community in the created work.[39] Although there is some distant historical truth in this argument, it is certainly no longer applicable.[40] The two approaches were effectively brought together in the Berne Convention, and the difference is little more than one of emphasis. Even so, that difference of emphasis is significant, and raises some interesting issues.

The central question concerns the purpose of copyright. From one point of view, intellectual property law exists to encourage intellectual innovation and to protect the innovator. The underlying principle is perhaps best illustrated by patent law, under which the inventor of a new material, process or device registers the invention, together with its design or formula, and the evidence of originality. Thereafter, the invention can only be used on payment of a royalty to the inventor. The 'inventor', of course, is at least as likely to be a company or some other corporate body (such as a university) as it is to be an individual. Especially in high profit industries, such as pharmaceuticals, patents are a vital form of capital representing the company's major investment in its future prosperity. The debate about the 'ownership' of human genetic code, as the Human Genome Project neared completion in mid-2000, exemplified the importance attached to such matters by scientists and business people. In essence, it was argued that without the protection afforded by intellectual property laws there would be no incentive to develop new ideas, especially if their development involved a significant financial cost. The just reward for successful investment lies in the profits to be made from exploiting the invention for a period of time after the patent is registered.

The same argument is applied to copyright in all media and formats. Intellectual and financial capital are invested in writing a book, making a movie or composing a piece of music. The creator (the 'author' in English legal terminology, whatever the actual form of the work) deserves an appropriate reward. How this reward is obtained is a matter of commercial convention rather than legal prescription. For example, in book publishing, it is normal for the author to receive a royalty of 10% of the revenue from the book obtained by the publisher to whom the copyright has been sold or licensed. The whole book publishing industry is built around the mutual interest of authors in making the works available to publishers and the need for publishers to obtain such works. In the non-print media, the position is more complicated, especially where the work can be made available in more than one medium or format. A pop video provides a good example of complexity. There is copyright in the music, the lyrics, the choreography, the sound track and the video production itself as well as in the performance. These will typically have been created by several, and perhaps many, people and will be handled by the production company and the agents or employers of the creators. Consider how the various products can be used. When a copy of the video or DVD is sold, some or all of those involved will receive a royalty payment.[41] If it is broadcast, a further royalty is payable. If the sound track is issued separately as a CD, a fee and subsequent royalties will be paid. The same is true if the sound track is used as part of a movie. The complexities are almost without limits, and underpin the economics of the music industry and the broadcasting media as well as book, newspaper and magazine publishing, and much of the world's sporting activity.

Sport

Sport deserves a particular mention in this context, since it neatly illustrates the potential reach of information policy. Since 1956, English law has recognized the rights of the producers of a sporting event to control the right to broadcast or record it in any way, whether directly (live television, for example) or indirectly (sound-only commentary on radio, whether live or not).[42] In the early years of television, sporting authorities, especially in the UK, but to a lesser extent elsewhere, were deeply suspicious of live broadcasting. They believed that it would diminish their capacity to attract people to watch the event itself. In fact, the exact opposite has proved to be the case. Sports that were once the preserve of small social elites, like tennis, have become major global entertainments. Sports that commanded little interest beyond a small circle of players, like snooker, have become media spectacles and their players media stars. The major team games – the various forms of football in particular, and baseball and basketball in the USA – have found themselves able to charge broadcasters millions of pounds or dollars for the right to broadcast important, and not so important, games. The broadcasters are only too happy to pay for this immensely popular entertainment; the success of News International's satellite television operation was largely built on it.[43] Money has poured into these sports, benefiting players, team owners and shareholders and even the game itself when some of this largesse is invested in promoting the sport and recruiting new participants and spectators.[44] The International Olympic Committee is perhaps the outstanding example of a governing body that has allowed its event to be dominated by the needs of the media and then come to depend on the income derived from television. The American network, NBC, paid $4 billion for the right to broadcast the Olympics and Winter Olympics from 1998 to 2008. In return it expects to have control over such matters as the timing of events (to coincide with peak viewing times in the USA) and, with the IOC, is working to prevent web-based competition developing.[45] We are perhaps not very far from the day when live spectators will be an irrelevance in an age of broadcast and webcast sporting events, unless they are the honoured guests of the corporate sponsors who want to see their logos on national and global television. In the meanwhile, global corporations piggyback on global television coverage to promote their own wares.[46]

We have devoted a paragraph to this aspect of sport because it exemplifies the widespread implications of intellectual property law in particular and information policy in general. In a society increasingly dominated by information and communications technologies, including broadcasting, information policy can impinge on almost any form of activity.

In general terms, copyright achieves two things: it punishes the illicit copying or dissemination of copyright material, and it allows promoters, innovators and creators to benefit from the results of their investment, intellect and ingenuity.

Data protection

Data protection is, in a sense, the mirror image of copyright, but unlike copyright with its early modern origins, it is very much a product of the age of the computer. The demand for data protection arises out of the recognition that computers allow governments, other public bodies and indeed private organizations to store vast quantities of data about individuals. The basic principle of data protection is that this data should be accurate and that it should be used only with the permission of the data subject and for the purpose for which it was collected. Legislation to this effect was first developed in Germany and Scandinavia in the 1970s, and had spread to most other democracies by the mid-1980s. Britain's first legislation was in 1984. The USA, where there is a traditional emphasis on freedom of access to information,[47] is unusual among democracies in having no such legislation at federal level.

The essence of the British Data Protection Act, and of the European Union directives and legislation to which it is related, is that data should be under the control of the data subject, that is the person to whom the information appertains.[48] The data subject typically has the right to know what data is held, and to verify its accuracy. When data is collected, the data subject has the right to be told that it will be held, and to restrict its use. At the same time, the holder of the data has an obligation to ensure that its confidentiality is protected, and it is used only for authorized purposes. To facilitate this, databases and, in some circumstances and some countries, paper-based records, must be registered, and data subjects must be made aware that information about them is held by the data owner. As with copyright, many complex practices, some of great commercial significance, have grown up around these basic principles, and have developed very quickly.

When supplying data, the data subject has the right to know why it is wanted and by whom it is being collected. A superficially simple example will illustrate the point. If a person buys an electrical product that brings with it a manufacturer's or retailer's warranty, ownership of the goods has to be registered for the warranty to take effect. This typically involves the purchaser in supplying his or her name, address (including postcode) and perhaps other details such as telephone number or e-mail address. This is, of course, entirely legitimate and for the genuine benefit of the data subject if the warranty has to be activated. The data owner, however, must seek the data subject's permission to use this data for any other purpose, such as adding his or her name to a mailing list for sending advertising material. Typically, however, the data subject must indicate that he or she does *not* want this to happen, a strange gap in legislation, which generally favours the rights of the data subject over those of the data owner. More insidiously, the data subject may also be giving implicit permission for information to be passed on to third parties who may also exploit it for commercial purposes. Again, he or she is required to refuse permission rather than to grant it.[49]

Junk mail generated from address lists is a nuisance; penetration of other personal data may be more dangerous. Perhaps the most sensitive areas are those of information about health and personal finances. Information about aspects of an individual's health is legitimately held by health-care professionals, including doctors, dentists and opticians. Typically, there is no central record, although a general medical practitioner would normally have information derived from any specialists to whom a patient has been referred. In 1990, patients in the UK were granted the right to read their own records (for a fee), under a piece of legislation against which the medical professionals had mounted a long battle.[50] This has at least forced doctors and others to be more cautious in some of their comments about patients. There are, however, others for whom access to the medical records of individuals would be advantageous. These include insurance companies, banks and employers. An individual must give permission before medical records can be released, and he or she has the right to see the report that is sent to the enquirer.[51] The patient's rights are in practice limited by the fact that in some circumstances services or employment may be refused if the this permission is not given or if the subject will not submit to a special medical examination. In effect, in seeking a job or a loan or insurance cover, an individual is forced to release personal data. Again that data is protected; it can be used only for the purpose for which it is intended. But the policing of data protection depends almost entirely on the good will of law-abiding data owners.

This is particularly important in the case of financial records. Credit-checking agencies have access to data from a wide range of institutions that lend money to individuals and companies. These include banks, building societies, loan companies, charge and credit card companies, and so on. Again, it is typically to the subject's benefit to allow the information to be made available, and to permit credit checks to be made. Credit may be refused if such permission is not given. In Britain, credit-checking agencies are controlled by legislation, but there is widespread suspicion of abuse of the system. A consultation about the relationship between data protection and credit checking was held in early 1999.[52]

Exceptions to data protection law are made for data that has some importance in terms of security or crime. The law in most countries allows the police or other security services to maintain files on individuals in certain circumstances and to gain access to normally confidential files when they suspect that a crime has been committed. A number of high-profile cases involving the records of banks in a number of countries have revealed the limits of such legislation and the extent to which it varies between countries. It is not only the offshore banking countries that have impenetrable laws, but also countries of the utmost respectability, such as Switzerland.[53]

Data protection is a very ambiguous tool. On the one hand, it is one of the ways in which the citizens of the information society can ensure that they are its beneficiaries rather than its victims. It protects personal privacy and affords some protection against unwanted soliciting by companies. It allows individuals to ensure that when information about them is recorded it is legitimate, accurate, current and fair. To that extent, it clearly protects the rights of individuals. On the other hand, data protection legislation is typically a compromise between the rights of individuals and needs and demands of business and the state. The need for the individual to intervene to prevent information being handed to other organizations exemplifies this. Out of all of this a significant sector of business has developed in trading in mailing lists. Advertising by selective mail shots has become more common, often using data derived from socio-economic studies of post codes to determine how recipients are selected. Abuses of data protection law are difficult to discover. Finally, much of the law, imperfect as it is, does not apply at all to the internet. Junk e-mail is only too familiar to regular users, and the very nature of the internet and the web make control over data exchange all but impossible.[54]

A consideration of the uncertainties and ambiguities of data protection law highlights a major dilemma for the makers of information policy. The law tries, however imperfectly, to keep some sort of balance between the rights of individuals on the one hand and legitimate business practices on the other. Its greatest challenge, however, comes from technological development. Data protection became a political issue because of the perception that data held on computers could be readily transferred from one owner to another. The perception is, of course, broadly true, and the transfer is infinitely easier now than it was 15 or 20 years ago. But technology and its applications continue to develop apace. Protection of data transmitted across the internet, or even data legitimately gathered by such means, is truly problematic. As with copyright, the law-makers are always following the technologists, trying to establish an orderly regime in a rapidly changing world. We shall return to this dilemma.[55]

Freedom of information

Freedom of information is also a concern that emerged in the last third of the 20th century from the growing public recognition of the potency of information and its ever-increasing importance in an information-driven world. Unlike the three areas of policy that we have discussed so far, freedom of information is specifically concerned with information generated and held by governments. The underlying philosophical principle is that there is a right of access to all such information, unless it can be proved (to the satisfaction of a court, if necessary) that there is good reason for withholding it. The pressure for such legislation has come not only from journalists (who are among its more obvious beneficiaries) but also from libertarian pressure groups of the left and the right who are inherently suspicious of governments. Such pressure is at all levels of government, from the supranational (such bodies as the European Commission) to the most low-level (the parish council in England and equivalent bodies elsewhere).

The USA was first in the field with comprehensive and powerful legislation in 1966, amended in 1996 to catch up with current technology. Many other democratic countries followed the US example in the 1970s.[56] The US system remains the most highly developed form of freedom of information legislation. All information generated by the US government is assumed to be in the public domain. If requested it must be released. It can be withheld only if the government can satisfy the courts that national security would be adversely affected if the information were published. This legislation has proved to be very powerful, although it has needed to be strengthened from time to time, notably in the aftermath of the presidency of Richard M. Nixon, who resigned in 1976 after the Watergate scandal. Older means, such as the use of the *sub poena*, had had to be used as the instruments which had forced him and others to reveal documents (and, famously, tapes) to the press and to Congress.[57] The law has, however, been used in a number of environmental *causes célèbres*, especially in the nuclear and petrochemical industries.[58] FOIA, as it is commonly known, has massively reinforced the tradition of investigative journalism that has characterized both the best and the worst of the US press since the age of the muckrakers.[59] It has even proved useful to people outside the USA, since there is no limit on who can apply for information under the Act. British journalists and others have benefited from this in a number of ways.[60]

The UK itself came late to this field. The first, and for many years only, legislation related solely to local government bodies. Under the Local Government (Access to Information) Act of 1985 local authorities were required to make available all committee papers and similar documents on which their decisions were based. There were exceptions for papers that contained commercially sensitive information or information about individuals. This law came from a right-wing government, and was largely intended as a political gesture against certain city councils, which the government considered to be dominated by politicians of the extreme left.[61] Moreover, in practice the legislation has proved more valuable in guaranteeing the public (and, perhaps more importantly, journalists) the right of attendance at committee meeting. Only in Autumn 2000 did parliament finally pass the Freedom of Information Act in the UK; even that is already being criticized as being inadequate and giving insufficient rights to citizens.[62]

Regulatory regimes: telecommunications and broadcasting

The regulation of public access telecommunications systems and broadcasting networks is a central element in information policy at the beginning of the 21st century. Although such regulations have been in existence since networks began to be developed in the late 19th century, it is only in the last 20 or so years that they have been identified as a dimension of information policy, and indeed seen as closely related to each other. This is partly a consequence of the possibility – now the reality – of technological convergence. In 1980, telecommunications were based on a hard wire network, with some microwave support through satellites for international communications. Broadcasting on the other hand was undertaken by radio wave transmission, sometimes supported locally by cable-based rediffusion. By 2000, all of that had changed. Telephony was increasingly based on radio transmission for the entire transaction. Cable broadcasting had expanded its scope, and direct satellite broadcasting was commonplace. Hard-wire telecommunications networks were regularly carrying multimedia digital signals, and genuinely interactive bi-directional television was a reality. It was no longer possible to distinguish between telecommunications providers and broadcasters in terms of the technologies of communication and delivery.[63]

At the same time, the political climate also changed dramatically. The neo-liberal economic policies pursued in most industrialized countries in the 1980s led to the loosening of regulatory regimes, especially in broadcasting, and the privatization of state-owned telecommunications corporations and in some case broadcasters as well. The declared intention of the politicians was to open up the systems to competition; this was only partially achieved. In both Britain and the USA, for example, the former monopolies continued to dominate the telecommunications markets, even though they did indeed have competitors. Their *de facto* control of the long-distance networks effectively ensured this.[64] Breaking the broadcasting monopolies and oligopolies was an easier nut for the politicians to crack. Licences were granted to new terrestrial channels and to new systems such as cable and satellite. In some cases (including the UK) the new entrants into broadcasting had less stringent conditions imposed on them than the privatized telecommunications companies, so that, for example, while they could offer telephony services, telecommunications companies could not offer entertainment services such as video on demand.[65]

The role that governments exercise in relation to this aspect of information policy is basically to grant licences to companies or public corporations, in the broader context of international agreements. These agreements control the use of wavelengths for broadcasting and the protocols for telecommunications systems, both analogue and digital. In most countries there is still a dominant telecommunications provider, although competition is increasingly common, as we have suggested. The traditional state-owned monopolies do survive in some places, but mainly in the developing countries. Even this is being challenged. The growth of mobile telephony, which is particularly valuable in countries or regions with an under developed telecommunications infrastructure, has led to the development of competition to the state providers even in countries where the monopoly for fixed line communications is still intact. The dilemma for governments is complex. A modern telecommunications system is necessary for every aspect of life and for economic and social development. The infrastructure, however, is expensive to provide and increasingly complex. Capital costs of development are a burden on strained economies in less developed countries, especially those with widely scattered and largely rural populations. To allow transnational companies to provide what the state cannot afford is an obvious and often irresistible alternative to slow development or no development. Across south-east Asia, in particular, where so many countries are hovering on the verge of industrialized status and developed economies, this has proved to be an important way forward.

The state's role in broadcasting

The state's role in broadcasting is an even more fraught – and highly politicized – area of information policy. With the partial exception of the USA, the regulation of broadcasting has always been about more than maintaining order in the use of wavelengths. In democratic states, the public provision of broadcasting is seen as providing a service on an equitable basis to all citizens. The building of transmitters, or of local cable systems to distribute the signals in areas where transmission is difficult or impossible, is thus provided at public expense. This was true, in effect, even in the UK, where the unique licensing system that has funded the BBC since its foundation in 1922 was a hypothecated tax on all owners of radio (and later television) receivers.[66] In many countries, of course, the monopoly state broadcasting systems was (and in some cases still is) an overt tool of government.

The less regulated systems that now prevail in all of the industrialized countries, and increasingly elsewhere, normally follow the American model of funding broadcasting from advertising and sponsorship. Governments have intervened in a number of aspects of this beyond merely allowing competition. Regulations may cover such matters as the maximum amount of advertising that is allowed, the products, goods and services that may be advertised (perhaps including a 'watershed' rule),[67] and the relationship between programme makers and programme sponsors. In a broader sense, there are in some cases residual 'public service' obligations to provide, for example, news bulletins. In the UK, the regime is still quite strict even for the commercial companies, which are regulated by the Independent Television Commission. When the principal commercial network moved its evening news bulletin, called News at Ten, from 10 p.m. to 11 p.m. in 1999, it became a major political issue provoking questions in parliament and a prolonged public debate. The BBC announced its intention to move its own main bulletin from 9 p.m. to 10 p.m., and several cable and satellite news channels (including the BBC's News 24) promoted the fact that they offered a 'news at ten'. In the late summer of 2000, ITN – the news franchisee responsible for News at Ten – responded to this mixture of public, political and commercial pressure by announcing the partial restoration of its 10 p.m. bulletin. It was all a striking illustration of how a fairly light regulatory regime can work when it has public and political support.[68] There is even a requirement that certain sporting events must be shown on a free-to-air terrestrial channel because they are deemed to be of national importance.[69]

Direct satellite broadcasting has, of course, changed this forever. The satellite companies are, in effect, extraterritorial, although they are subject to some controls about what they can broadcast to particular countries.[70] There are, however, almost no controls over advertising or sponsorship, and no public service requirements. Governments have effectively lost control over what can be broadcast, and indeed what must be broadcast, in their national territories. In China, the response has been to try to control the reception of satellite television (by restricting the sales of equipment) and to encourage the development of cable, which is easier to control. Even there, success has only been partial.

Governments, however, have not completely lost control of broadcasting. Many have chosen to withdraw from it either wholly in part. There remain, however, key areas of information policy that surround broadcasting, and which remain to be resolved. Perhaps the most important of these is a direct consequence of technological convergence. Given the multiple capacities of both broadcasting and telecommunications systems, to what extent should commercial monopolies be allowed to develop that have significant interests in both fields? The question becomes an even more urgent one when we realize that the major global companies in the field also have vast interests in newspapers, publishing and the internet. News Corporation (formerly News International) is perhaps the archetype of this trend towards cross-media ownership; its interests include newspapers, film and video production, terrestrial and satellite television production and broadcasting, book publishing and radio, and, through alliances and subsidiaries, audio CD production and marketing, and data base development and distribution. It operates on every continent and in most countries. Moreover, News Corporation is only one of several companies on this scale and with this scope, and it is not the largest.[71] The shape of the future is suggested by the recent takeover of Time-Warner, the world's largest media corporation and heir to some of the most venerable names in book publishing and film production, by America On Line, a youngster of barely 20 years, which was not even the largest of the ISPs. The combined company immediately became the world's largest or second largest operator in every market in which it traded.[72]

Access to information

The recognition of the economic and social benefits that flow from efficient and easy access to information has been a key influence in policy development in areas that are somewhat removed from information itself. It is too easy to see the role of governments, and of their information policies, as being restrictive and inhibiting. This is far from being the case, and some of this has brought information policy closer to the centre of the political debate than has ever formerly been the case. The need for education and training has been highlighted by the development of the internet, and in particular by its potential as an educational tool in its own right. School curricula are being radically revised to ensure that children are familiarized with the use of computers from an early age. Information technology was introduced, as a separate subject, into the national school curriculum in England in 1995.[73] The problem appears to be in finding enough teachers competent to deal with the subject rather than in arousing the children's interest in it. Similarly, public provision has been made for adults who wish to enhance and develop their skills, or indeed who wish to learn from scratch.[74] The basic skills of computer use, however, are only one of the educational gaps that have been opened up by the development of information and communications technologies and the demands of an information society.

In the industrialized countries sophisticated telecommunications networks and readily available hardware and software make the use of computers and access to networks easy. More precisely, it is available to everyone who can afford it. This is the policy dilemma that faces governments. ICT could too easily become – perhaps has already become – another instrument of social and economic divisiveness from which those who might be its most important beneficiaries are excluded. The French government recognized this as long ago as the late 1970s. When broadcasting networks and telecommunications corporations throughout the world were introducing pioneering videotext services (such as PRESTEL and CEEFAX in the

UK), the French telephone provider (a state monopoly) gave every subscriber a free terminal (MINITEL) from which to access its system, TELETEL. This unique experiment in social engineering by technology actually made TELETEL probably the only successful videotext system in the world.[75] So far, no government has repeated this experiment using PCs and modems, although provision of ICT in schools is a major item of public expenditure on education in most industrialized countries.

The alternative method, which has been widely adopted, has been to provide public access PCs through which members of the public can access the internet or avail themselves of other computing facilities. The rapid development of internet cafés in the late 1990s was perhaps the most visible symbol of this. They were usually commercial enterprises, but public service providers imitated them. The most obvious institutions through which provision could be made were public libraries. Although developments have been uneven, this is now widely recognized by librarians, and public libraries in many places are providing access to the internet, sometimes charged but sometimes with some initial free time and perhaps some training.[76] Public access is not, however, confined to libraries, and is increasingly common across all public services. Perhaps the most radical development in the United Kingdom has been the so-called University for Industry (UfI) whose Learn Direct network is intended to provide facilities for life long learning for everyone outside the formal education system.[77]

The potential cost of this aspect of information policy to government is immense. Moreover, it is, as we have suggested, far beyond the scope of information policy as it has been traditionally understood. Yet it also shows that information policy can no longer be confined to those matters which clearly have a direct and obvious relevance to the storage and dissemination of information. It impinges on education and social welfare – historically high spending and politically sensitive areas – as well as on more obviously information-related matters such as public library provision. The whole question of public access remains essentially unresolved, and will be a major policy issue for the present decade.[78]

The pervasiveness of information in the knowledge-based economy of the late 20th century has forced a reconsideration of the domain of information policy and role that governments should play. During the 1990s, governments became increasingly concerned to ensure that individuals and organizations were not disadvantaged by lack of access to information that would be beneficial to them. In the USA, this took the form of encouraging the development of the so-called information superhighway, a network that would facilitate internet access. This has been taken forward by legislation that facilitates development by deregulation, but the real drivers are commercial.[79] The British version has been to support the networking of universities, schools and public libraries. In practice, governments have done little more than facilitate. The vast growth of the internet – 25% of British households now have access, in addition to access through the workplace, places of education and so on – has been driven by individuals and facilitated by the private sector. The role of government seems to be to encourage, to educate and to ensure that deprivation is minimized, while actively supporting developments in sectors that are not commercially attractive.[80]

The informed citizen

Governments collect and generate vast quantities of information; indeed it is the awareness of this that has driven the demand for legislation on both data protection and freedom of information. They may seek to disseminate much of this information on such matters as social security entitlements, and this too is an increasingly important dimension of information policy. The public's right to know is satisfied not merely by legislation that gives a right to answers to questions, but by active policies to make information available through various channels. This partly reflects the increasing demand for information from individuals as citizens. In part, this has grown out of the consumer movement (which itself could be argued to be a product of the information society), which has come to form such an important pressure group in most western countries in the last 20 years. The demand for information is insistent; governments that are dependent on the support of their electorates, however reluctantly in some cases, are obliged to develop policies to satisfy it.

Conclusion

In this chapter, we have tried to introduce some key issues and fundamental facts about information policy. The complexity and comprehensiveness of the subject has led us into many different spheres. That is as it should be. The information society is an all-embracing concept. It means different things to different people, and perhaps it always will. We can, however, perhaps see some sort of pattern by trying to pull together the work of information scientists, information theorists, computer scientists, technologists, sociologists, economists, political scientists and even politicians.

Knowledge and information have always been fundamental to human activity. In the last half-century, however, the systematic study of information has enabled us to define more clearly the relationship between knowledge, economic activity and the social and political consequences of economic activity. The development of revolutionary new technologies for the storage, processing and communication of information has added a new dimension to the knowledge-based activities of human beings. Long-established political, social and economic traditions are being overturned under the global impact of the new systems for the communication of information. Governments throughout the world have been forced to develop policies that meet these new circumstances. While some of their traditional powers decline, especially in the economic sphere, they are faced with insistent demand to provide access to information and to alleviate the causes and consequences of information deprivation. Much of this is still far from fully understood. The information society is so difficult to define, and so many definitions can be cogently offered, precisely because it is still evolving, and what we see now, and what we can learn from the past, is only an imperfect guide to its future development.

Information policy is not, however, only concerned with carefully defined legal rights or restrictions on the circulation and dissemination of information; it is concerned with much more than the provision of a legal and regulatory framework within which information can be stored and disseminated. In its broadest sense, as it is increasingly understood in practice, information policy addresses the positive issues that arise out of technological change and the perceived development of an information society. In various countries, there are powerful examples of how, with greater or lesser success, governments and international organizations can harness the power for information technology for the good of society as a whole. We have referred to such matters as the development of information super-highway in the USA, British efforts to bring the internet into all schools and to use it for the provision of health information and life-long learning, and the French government's pioneering provision of teletext services. On a much wider scale, however, governments are now trying to generalize from these specific experiences, and to develop policies that will actually drive forward the development of the information society as a whole. Nowhere is this more marked than in the European Union, whose policies, along with those of some other states, we shall consider in Chapter 5.

A note on further reading

The basic principles and domain of information policy are explored in Montviloff (note 20). On specific aspects, see the Aslib guide (note 38) on copyright, Davies (note 54) on data protection, the websites of the Campaign for Freedom of Information (note 62) and Index on Censorship (note 25) on their respective topics, and the work of Herman and McChesney (see note 24 to Chapter 3, p. 59) and Baldwin, McVoy and Steinfeld across the whole field (see note 15 to Chapter 2, p. 40), but especially in relation to the mass media. Many of the issues we cover in this chapter are on the political agenda in various countries; intelligent reading of serious newspapers will reveal a good deal about many of them.

Notes and references

1 For a study of the general issue, see Trevor Haywood, *Info-rich, info-poor: access and exchange in the global information society*, Bowker-Saur, 1997.
2 *Nua internet surveys: 1996 review* at
   http://www.nua.ie/surveys/1996review.html
3 Tom Butterly, Constraints in the development of the 'wired' economy in Africa, available at
   http://www.nua.ie/surveys/analysis/africa_analysis.html
   There is a good discussion of the whole issue in Everard, 30–4.
4 Herman and McChesney, 133.

5 Tawfik, *World communication and information report*, Table A1.

6 Butterly, as cited in note 3, above.

7 Giddens, *Third way*, 28. The first British usage of the word recorded in the *Oxford English Dictionary* is from the magazine *The Spectator* in 1962. The journalist described it as a 'staggering concept'.

8 Castells, *Rise of the network society*, 66–147.

9 See, for example, Organisation for Economic Co-operation and Development. *Globalisation of industrial activities. Four case studies: auto parts, chemicals, construction and semi-conductors*, OECD, 1992.

10 Reported, for example, in *The Guardian*, 12 August 2000, 15. The sites at issue are auctions of Nazi memorabilia; trading in such goods is forbidden under French law. There was a threat of a $13,000 a day fine, but it is unclear how this could have been enforced. The issue was resolved when Yahoo! itself decided to ban trading in these goods from its online auction sites. See David Usborne, Yahoo! To ban trade in racist material on website, *Independent*, 4 January 2001, 12.

11 Herman and McChesney, 51.

12 The most obvious case is that of the use of tax havens by companies and individuals to protect their wealth and to inhibit regulation. Banking in the Cayman Islands or the registration of shipping in Liberia are two of the most familiar examples. Both, of course, long predate the development of the internet, and the examples reiterate the importance of avoiding a simplistic equation of the internet and globalization.

13 Mark Findlay, *The globalisation of crime: understanding transitional relationships in context*, Cambridge University Press, 1999.

14 See, for example, Giddens, *Third way*, 28–33; Castells, *Power of identity*, 243–308; Paul Kennedy, *Preparing for the twenty-first century*, Fontana, 1994, 47–64; and Anthony Giddens, *Runaway world: how globalisation is reshaping our lives*, Profile Books, 1999.

15 Castells, *Rise of the network society*, 201–79.

16 A British minister suggested in September 2000 that the UK's very strict laws on immigration needed to be amended to facilitate the recruitment of such workers. The outcry was less strident than might have been expected by those familiar with the history of immigration into the UK since 1960. Barbara Roche's

initiative was widely reported in the British press between 9 and
11 September 2000. A very practical example arose in the winter
of 2000–1 when Railtrack, the company responsible for the maintenance of the national railway network, was forced to bring in
engineers and engineering workers from Italy and even India to
undertake an emergency programme of major repairs. Again, this
was widely reported in the press. See also below, p. 102.

17 For a thoughtful view from the left, see Patricia Hewitt, Social
inclusion in the information society, *RSA Journal,* **2** (4), 1998,
97–101.

18 Charles Oppenheim and Noreen MacMorrow, in Feather and
Sturges, 198.

19 See John C. Gray, *National information policies: problems and
progress*, Mansell, 1988.

20 Victor Montviloff, *National information policies: a handbook on the
formulation, approval, implementation and operation of a national
policy on information.* Paris: UNESCO, 1990 (PGI-90/WS/11),
offers the following definition: 'guidance for the design of a
strategy and programme for the development and use of information resources, services and systems . . . a set of such policies
. . . at the institutional, national, regional or international level'
(p..7).

21 John Milton, *Areopagitica*, 1644.

22 John Feather, *A history of British publishing*, Routledge, 1988,
88–92.

23 See Richard D. Brown, The shifting freedoms of the press in the
eighteenth century. In Hugh Amory and David D. Hall (eds), *A
history of the book in America. Volume I, The colonial book in this
Atlantic world*, Cambridge University Press, 2000, 366–7.

24 It is more difficult, by definition, to give examples of this hid-
den practice, but the cautious, indeed often obsequious, references to the Thai royal family in the newspapers of that country
is certainly one case in point.

25 For a survey of the current state of the freedom of the press,
regularly updated with examples, see the *Index on censorship* website at
http://www.indexoncensorship.org/ii/iiintro.html

26 For the development of the American system, see Robert W.

McChesney, *Telecommunications, mass media and democracy: the battle for the control of U.S. broadcasting 1927–1935*, Oxford University Press, 1993.

27 In practice, this means sanitized sex and strictly rationed and selected obscene language. There is no pornography on the free-to-view channels in Britain; in language, 'fuck' is now heard frequently on television, 'cunt' virtually never. In writing this note, we observe that the former is in the dictionary of the Word 98 spell checker, while the latter is not!

28 See David A. L. Levy, *Europe's digital revolution: broadcasting regulation, the European Union and the nation state*, Routledge, 1999, 173, note 9.

29 Paul H. Henry, Roscoe 'Fatty' Arbuckle, 1994, a fully documented paper, at
http://www.halcyon.com/phenry/text/arbuckle.tex

30 For the original version of the Code, see
http://www.artsreformation.com/a001/hays-code.html

31 David Fisher, British film and video censorship and classification, at
http://www.terramedia.co.uk/themes/british_film_censorship.htm
For the current position, see Alan Travis, *Bound and gagged: a secret history of obscenity in Britain*, Profile Books, 2000, 272–89.

32 Everard, 135–8.

33 Everard, 141–9.

34 Everard, 37–8, 60.

35 See John Feather, *Publishing, piracy and politics: an historical study of copyright in Britain*, Mansell, 1994; and Benjamin Kaplan, *An unhurried view of copyright*, Columbia University Press, 1967.

36 Debora J. Halbert, *Intellectual property in the information age: the politics of expanding ownership rights*, Quorum Books, 1999, 25–76.

37 Or, in certain circumstances, their employers.

38 *The Aslib guide to copyright*, Aslib, 1994, with its regular loose-leaf updates, is probably the best practical guide.

39 Carla Hesse, Enlightenment epistemology and the laws of authorship in pre-Revolutionary France, *Representations*, **30**, 1998, 109–37.

40 Jane C. Ginsbury, A tale of two copyrights: literary property in revolutionary France and America, *Tulane Law Review*, **64**, 1990, 991–1031; see also the comments in Feather, *Publishing, piracy and politics*, 3–4.

41 This will almost certainly be true of the performers, the composer and the lyricist. The others involved are more likely to be paid employees of the performers or the production company.

42 Feather, *Publishing, piracy and politics*, 204–5.

43 Herman and McChesney, 75–7.

44 On soccer in the UK and Europe, see Levy, 83–4. For an American comment, see Baldwin, McVoy and Steinfeld, 157, note 17.

45 On the restrictions on webcasting, as well as on more general matters, see Sean Dodson and Patrick Barkham, Why the net is not invited to Sydney, *Guardian*, 14 September 2000, Online, 2–3.

46 See, for example, Richard Williams, Let the MacGames begin, *Guardian*, 9 September 2000, accessible on **http://www.observer.co.uk/Guardian/sydney/story/0,7369, 366355,00.html**

47 See below, p. 77.

48 We deal with the complexities of EU information policies in Chapter 5.

49 A typical formula, which we take at random from a piece of junk mail that arrived on the day this sentence was written reads: 'From time to time we permit other companies which must be registered under the Data Projection Act to write to you about their products. If you would prefer not to hear from such companies, please tick the box marked *.'
This statement is in 6-point type!

50 Access to Health Records Act, 1990.

51 This right has been in place since the Access to Medical Reports Act, 1988.

52 See Dept of Trade and Industry, *Consumers' access to their credit reference files under the Data Protection Act 1988*. DTI, 1999 (also available at **http://www.dti.gov.uk/cacp/ca/cacref.htm**).
The key UK statute is the Consumer Credit Act of 1974. For the rather different position in the USA, see Federal Reserve Sys-

tem, *Consumer handbook to credit protection laws*, Governors of the Federal Reserve System, 1993.

53 We have in mind, for example, the well-publicized cases involving the bank accounts of former Nazis and their sympathizers and supporters outside Germany; and cases in which suspected financial irregularities by individuals or companies could not be investigated because of legislation in the countries in which accounts were held or companies were registered.

54 See Davies, J. E., *Data protection: a guide for library and information management*, Elsevier, 1984, for a good general introduction to British law. For the current position, see the Data Protection Agency's website at **http://dataprotection.gov.uk**.

55 See below, p. 139.

56 For a current (and frequently updated) account, see David Banisar, Freedom of information around the world, at **http://www.privacyinternational.org/issues/foia/foia-survey.html**.

57 Michael Schudra, *Watergate in American memory*, Basic Books, 1992, 99–100; Theodore H. White, *Breach of faith: the fall of Richard Nixon*, Atheneum Publishers, 1975, 295.

58 For examples of requests made under the Freedom of Information Act, see, for example, the US National Parks website at **http://www.nps.gov/refdesk/hotdocs.htm**.

59 See Harry H. Stein and John M. Harrison, Muckraking journalism in twentieth-century America. In John M. Harrison and Harry H. Stein, *Muckraking: past, present and future*, University of Pennsylvania Press, 1974, 11–22.

60 Some interesting examples are quoted on the Campaign for Freedom of Information's website at **http://cfoi.org.uk/usfoiapr/htm**

61 See Hugo Young, *One of us: a biography of Margaret Thatcher*, Pan, 1989, 538–9.

62 For the legislation, see **www.publications.parliament.uk/ ld199900/ldbills/055/2000055.htm** For the views of the pressure group, the Freedom of Information Campaign, see

http://www.cfoi.org.uk

63 See above, pp. 37–8.

64 There is a useful introductory summary, largely American in perspective but politically neutral in tone, in Baldwin, McVoy and Steinfeld, 301–52.

65 For an account of the British experience, by two distinguished American scholars, see Herman and McChesney, 166–70.

66 Asa Briggs, *The BBC: the first fifty years*, Oxford University Press, 1988, 30–1.

67 For the 'watershed' concept, see above, p. 66.

68 This whole episode was the subject of much publicity. For a useful summary, see Matt Wells, Back with a bong, and Maggie Brown, A matter of timing, both in the *Guardian*, 25 September 2000, Media, 2–5. The BBC began its 10 p.m. bulletins on 16 October 2000.

69 This is protected under the Broadcasting Act 1996; a revised list was produced in 1997–8, which includes the Olympics, Wimbledon, and the World Cup finals in cricket, rugby and soccer.

70 See above, pp. 66–7.

71 For an excellent analysis, see Herman and McChesney, 70–105, which includes a detailed discussion of News Corporation, 70–7.

72 The deal was finally approved by the American and European regulatory authorities in December 2000 after almost a year of uncertainty. See Amy Vickers, AOL Time Warner merger through. *Media Guardian*, 14 December 2000, available at **http://www.mediaguardian.co.uk/city/story/00,7497,411534,00. html**
For the background, see Peter Spiegel, Regulations out of step on issue of the internet, *Financial Times*, 13–14 January 2001, 20.

73 Dept for Education, *The National Curriculum: England*, DfE, 1995, vi.

74 We deal with this at greater length in Chapter 6.

75 Baldwin, McVoy and Steinfield, 65.

76 See Peter Stone, Catherine Hume and Peter Smith, *Project EARL (Electronic Access to Resources in Libraries): networking for public libraries' information and resource sharing services via the Internet. Final Report*, The British Library (BLRDD Innovation Report, 42), 1997. For a broad strategic overview, see John Dolan, Uphill

and down dale: citizens, government and the public library. In Sally Criddle, Lorcan Dempsey, L. and Richard Heseltine (eds), *Information landscape for a learning society: networking and future of libraries 3*, Library Association Publishing, 1999, 133–44.

77 For the most advanced UfI scheme, see **http://www.learning.org.uk/frameset.htm**

78 See also below, p. 145.

79 Baldwin, McVoy and Steinfeld, 302–3.

80 It has been cogently argued that the need for active government intervention is acute in less developed countries; the argument is still valid. See Katz, 47–79.

5

The information society in practice: the European experience

Introduction

Information policy can no longer be confined by national boundaries. This has been recognized since the signing of the Berne Convention in 1886 effectively internationalized the law of copyright. By the end of the 20th century, however, the ease of international communications, and the globalization of the developed economies, meant that national boundaries could no longer contain what were essentially international phenomena. Knowledge-driven economies resemble each other, just as economies based on extraction and manufacture were fundamentally similar despite their social and political differences. Similarly, the problems that arise from the universal use of identical technologies, and especially from global access to the internet (notably those of control of undesirable material), are notoriously evasive of national regulatory regimes. Information policies have followed information technology into the international arena, although often slowly and uncertainly.

At the same time, governments have recognized that information policy is about more than merely regulating the availability of information and to some extent regulating the information market place itself. Across the world, it has been understood that there are economic and social benefits to be derived from the use of information and communications technologies, as well as less desirable consequences (such as unemployment in traditional industries), which have also to be addressed. The positive approach is to encourage the development of an information society and to promote the use of ICT to support it. At national level, this is to be seen in such phenomena as the 'information superhighway' whose promotion was such a feature of the early years of the Clinton presidency in the USA. It can be seen too in the British government initiatives that have led to the creation of the People's Network based on public libraries. Network provision in both countries, however, has in practice been largely by the private sector, as might have been expected, although in the UK there have been notable public–private partnerships. Information policy thus takes on a more positive aspect, promoting the information society and the new economy that sustains it. It is in such initiatives that we can best see what this new society (if it is indeed truly new) looks like, and will perhaps look like in the future.

The process of encouraging the development of an information society is far advanced in western Europe, at least at the level of the European Union (EU).[1] In this chapter, we shall use the example of the EU to show how intervention can promote the development of an information society, and the limitations by which it is constrained. We shall begin by considering the political and economic context that caused the EU to identify the creation of an information society as an objective of policy. We then turn to a more or less chronological account of developments, beginning with the first faltering steps in the late 1980s. In the mid-1990s, the EU entered into a long-term commitment to the support of the infrastructure of the information society, expressed in the work of Commission President Jacques Delors, and his Vice-President, Martin Bangemann. In the retreat from the high tide of centralization towards the end of the century, new objectives were defined in terms of social inclusion and the fostering of new skills for social and cultural purposes as well as for wealth creation. Our account is not comprehensive. There are many aspects of policy that we do not touch on. We have tried to concentrate on the central themes as defined by the EU itself.

The story illustrates both the challenges and the difficulties of creating the circumstances in which an information-dependent society can flourish. It shows that technology alone is not enough; it shows that social consequences must be identified and addressed; and it shows that governments and the private sector will have to work together to achieve the full benefits of technological change. This grand declaration of intent was made in February 2000:

> A key aim will be to modernize Europe's economies and equip both citizens and the workforce with the skills needed in an on-line, Information Society. In stimulating the shift to a digital economy, a major contribution is likely to be made through the realization of President Prodi's Europe Initiative.[2]

Cynics might feel that the rhetorical flourishes are only too typical of its origin. In this chapter, we shall explore the realities, the successes and the shortcomings of Europe's progress into the digital age.

Moving to a model Europe?

Background

The evolution of the 'common market' of six countries envisaged in the Treaty of Rome in 1957 into the European Union of 15 states in 2001 was one of the most profound political changes of the second half of the 20th century.[3] Countries that had been at war with each other, or in unstable and shifting alliances for centuries, have found a common sense of purpose and begun to define a common destiny. The debate about where Europe is heading, and how and how quickly it should get there, is still very much alive, but the essential infrastructure of large-scale and high-level co-operation is in place. Since the early 1970s, following the first phase of expansion (which brought the UK, Ireland and Denmark into the European Community, as it was then called), the Community has been pursuing research and development projects designed to modernize social and economic activities at national and European levels. Programmes such as ESPRIT were intended to enhance Europe's capacity to produce, develop and exploit 'new technologies' (as they were then typically called), and led to a series of initiatives in the field of ICT, some of which are now bearing fruit.

The European Union of the early 21st century is not only focusing on the technology of information. There is a clear desire to develop an information society based on creating and developing a 'common information area', which uses interlinked ICT services, networked infrastructure and common content within the Community. This encompasses:

* information in digital format
* physical infrastructures such as cable, radio and satellite
* computer hardware and software
* universal access to telecommunications networks and services
* providing the user with access to specific information.

The development of the European Union's information society policy, and the development of the common information area since 1993, have been based on the assumption that ICT can be harnessed to generate economic growth and promote social cohesion. What the Commission calls the 'new industrial revolution' for European industry is also intended to generate knock-on effects in terms of education, training, employment and sustainability. This wide-ranging policy perhaps inevitably contains some contradictions, which are reflected in the strategies and policies adopted between 1993 and 2000. The early emphasis on developing effective ICT for Europe was followed by a shift at the end of the century towards policies designed to promote greater social inclusion. However, it is also obvious that the widespread uptake of ICT in the 1990s has made it possible, as well as timely and necessary, to develop a more broadly based information society policy. At the same time, in the background to this, as to all European policies, is the continuing tension between those who favour greater centralization and those who favour a distributed model of federalism. This tension exists between states, within states and indeed within political parties. No EU policy is immune from its consequences.[4]

The European Union approach

As we shall see, information society policy and initiatives in the EU have generally developed a twin-track approach, although with links between them:

- *bottom-up initiatives* developed by individual member states, and in some cases as joint initiatives between regions and member states in the EU (notably the various regional information society initiatives in the 1990s, known as IRISI, RISI and ERISA);[5]
- *top-down strategies* and initiatives formulated by the Commission, usually after substantive discussion and debate with other EU institutions, notably the Parliament and the Council of Ministers, as well as with and between member states themselves.

EU information society policy, like the Union itself, is a strange mixture of centralization and decentralization. Member states and their regions are encouraged to develop their own policies to serve their own specific needs. At the same time, the Commission has played a significant role since 1993 in terms of strategy, policy and standardization across the Union. The Commission has also taken on a more outward-looking role, recognizing that the information society and its underpinning technology is essentially global. This is exemplified, as we shall see, in such actions as the 'Bangemann Challenge' and in joint projects with Japan.[6]

The development of an information society in the EU has depended on generating synergy from the tensions between centralization and decentralization. It is recognized that information society policies are only likely to be successful when they are developed for specific needs in particular states or regions. On the other hand, successful policies implemented in one or two states have an obvious potential to impact on other member states, if only as examples of good practice. Therefore, it can be argued that information society policies in all member states will benefit from a wider and more focused approach including EU-level strategies, financial incentives, and the support of the Fourth and Fifth Framework programmes undertaken in the 1990s and collaboration with other parts of the Union.[7]

The rationale for a European information society policy

The problems faced by the European Union in further developing an information society were, and remain, substantial, and need to be explored. The most fundamental is the nature of the Union and indeed of Europe as a whole. Europe is not homogenous; indeed its historical heterogeneity lies at the root of the political debate about the future of the EU itself. The Union is a culturally and linguistically diverse area. In this respect, promoting a harmonized information society policy presents difficulties that do not impede single-language and largely culturally homogeneous countries such as Japan, or the culturally diverse but linguistically unified USA. The Union has 13 official languages, although English and French are probably the two most widely used, and English is, of course, dominant in the ICT sector throughout the world. The cultural diversity of the member states, moreover, is not likely to homogenize; indeed, regional policies positively encourage it, and the further growth of the EU planned for 2002 and again probably for 2005 will be another diversifying factor. Problems will be faced in integrating new member states, including former socialist countries, into the Union. There are significant obstacles to developing and maintaining a cohesive information society policy for a total population of over 300 million people at different levels of economic prosperity, social development and technological competence.

The EU has a complex administrative structure of its own, superimposed on an existing range of local, regional and national governance. Traditions vary greatly between member states. Germany, for example, has a decentralized federal system. Spain has regions with different levels of independence from central government, some of which (notably Catalonia and the Basque Country) are virtually autonomous for all domestic purposes. France is decentralizing, but has a strong centralist tradition; the same is true of the UK. The diversity of relationships between central and local governments, and the division of power between them, is a complicating factor in the relationships between the Union and its member states, as well as between the member states and each other. The desire of most member states is to preserve linguistic and cultural traditions even at subnational level. This coincides with the desire of a number of significant cultural minorities for decentralization, self-government and perhaps even severance of ties with their present nation states. This phenomenon is to be observed not only in Spain (Catalonia) and the UK (Scotland), where it has enjoyed some success, but also in

France (Brittany) and Italy (Lombardy) where so far it has not.

The EU's own emphasis on regions has forced some countries (notably the UK and France) to reconsider their own regional policies. Information policies driven by the Commission reach into member states at different levels, and to some extent depend on the willingness and ability of national governments to adopt and enforce them. To compound these issues, even without further expansion (which will happen), there are already significant problems in integrating poorer regions of the EU into a cohesive European information society policy. There is a real need to combat the apparent north–south divide in Europe, just as there is on a global scale.

These factors, which are inevitable but surmountable obstacles to integration, are exacerbated by negative public attitudes. There is a significant mixture of rejection, cynicism and apathy towards 'Europe' among many European citizens. There is indeed reluctance in some member states to take part in the full economic union to which they are committed by treaty, exemplified by the well-documented scepticism about the EU in the UK and Denmark. Although this is most often associated with the UK, where it is arguably derived from a long tradition of dislike of continental Europe as a whole by part of the political class, it is present in other states as well. There is a widespread perception across the whole Union (not least by politicians and civil servants) that the European institutions are at best bureaucratic, and at worst corrupt and toothless.

Against this background, developing meaningful policies for the promotion of a concept as vague as the 'information society' was never going to be easy. Harmonization of existing national laws is somewhat simpler, even if not uncontroversial. Thus key areas of information policy, such as copyright, are already essentially internationalized under earlier treaties and conventions.[8] The status of others is less clear; in particular, national legislation on data protection, freedom of information and censorship may well be subject to overriding European legislation in due course, and plans are already being developed to extend copyright law to give greater protection to the rights of authors.[9] Regulatory regimes for telecommunications and broadcasting are in a similar limbo. Nevertheless, it is possible to see how laws might be brought into line with each other, and with over-arching European law.

The development of an information society in Europe

An analysis and understanding of the European approach is further complicated by some of the issues we have raised in Chapter 1 about the very idea of an 'information society'. The EU concept, as we shall see, has been very much that the information society is ICT-based and that the creation and maintenance of an ICT infrastructure is fundamental to its development and sustenance. There is a far less well-developed idea of a 'knowledge-driven' or 'knowledge-based' society in the EU, perhaps reflecting the greater cultural difficulties to be encountered in attempts to bring together attitudes rather than technologies.

The EU's interest in the development of an information society had its origin, like the Union itself, in economic policies. This was made explicit by Jacques Delors, as President of the Commission, one of the great advocates of full integration between member states. In 1993, he was unambiguous: 'The one and only reason [for developing the information society policy] is unemployment.'[10] The European Union's information society policy stemmed from a desire to develop and maintain competitiveness with the USA and Japan, and to develop and sustain an ICT-based society that did not need to rely solely on the USA and Japan for ICT products. The Bangemann Report of 1994 was specific on this point: 'Why the urgency? Because competitive suppliers of networks and services from outside Europe are increasingly active in our markets.'[11]

Global competitiveness and economic growth within the member states have always been the drivers of the European Union. The Commission's decision to promote an 'information society' in the 1990s was a response to high levels of unemployment, which were due in part to the relative decline of primary and secondary heavy industries and the global challenge from knowledge-based activities. The consequent social impact – social deprivation and the growth of an information-poor underclass – reverberated across Europe. Although the Commission reported unemployment running at 11% in 1992, and it has continued to range between 8 and 13%, the huge growth of ICT employment in Europe during the 1990s revealed another, very different, labour market problem – a serious shortage of skilled professionals. Therefore, one of the areas to be tackled is training and educating professionals to work in the information society. At the same time, Europe is expected to experience a decrease in the growth-rate of its population during the 21st century, which will have the effect of producing an ageing population. It is estimated that by 2040, 34% of the European Union's 360 million citizens will be aged over 60 (compared with 15% aged under 20). Therefore, not only is there an employment problem for sustaining an ICT-based information society in Europe, there is also a need to accommodate an ageing population within this society, not least by ensuring that it includes the provision of services for the elderly and in support of healthcare.

An ICT-led information society also raises significant problems which a strong information society policy will have to address. If society is indeed to be transformed in a way that makes it reliant on electronic communications, everyone will need to be able to access the systems. This includes those who are currently unable to afford to do so, or do not have the necessary skills, or are physically disabled. The challenge is a huge one. While it is not unique to the EU, the dilemmas faced by the Union in going down its chosen road illustrate vividly the problems faced at both national and global levels. The sheer size of the EU, and its political, social and cultural diversity, will force it to find solutions to these problems if it is not to create a new underclass of the excluded.

The growth of ICT has itself created jobs although not all of these are the highly skilled professional and managerial occupations envisaged by the creators of the EU's information society initiatives, and indeed by Machlup and Porat.[12] Many of the new jobs are poorly paid, such as work in call centres. Because of the comparatively high cost of skilled and even semi-skilled labour in Europe and North America, much of the manufacturing sector of the ICT industry has moved to Korea, the Philippines and elsewhere in Asia where the assembly of computers and other hardware can be done more cheaply for a global market. At the same time, the EU itself is, as we have seen, suffering from a shortage of higher-level skills, and is beginning to import a skilled workforce from India and Malaysia.[13] The information society has many ramifications; as Castells has so eloquently reminded us, not the least of these are for the international labour market.[14]

The rapid development of the internet and speed of uptake of ICT has also raised problems of information overload and the variable quality of the information that is available.[15] Policies designed to promote the information society must therefore take account of the balance between moving rapidly to achieve competitiveness and employment, and moving so rapidly as to sacrifice both through a reputation for low quality.[16] The EU's policies are specifically aimed at developing an information-based society in the Union, which will facilitate competition with the Asian countries of the Pacific rim and the USA. In manufacturing, much ground has already been lost; the member states must therefore compete by making their knowledge creation generate wealth. At the same time, the Union has social policies that are designed to combat social exclusion and regional disadvantage. All the dangers inherent in the gaps between rich and poor, which the internet can exacerbate, are present within the EU itself. We have already noted the danger of a growing north–south divide in western Europe; to this we should add that there are economically and socially disadvantaged people in all the member states, even the wealthiest, and that all states have regions that have historically been less favoured. The justification for the EU's information policies and its thrust towards the development of a European information society is precisely that these disadvantages will be addressed, not that they will be continued.

The global nature of the changes symbolized by the internet makes the position even more complicated. Ideally, it might be argued that information society policies should benefit from a world consensus rather than becoming reliant on policies developed at a national or European level. In practice, competition makes this unlikely and perhaps even impossible. Europe must find its own solutions, and the European Commission is seeking to do so through the promotion of a networked economy across the European Union. Moreover, it must do this in a political context in which, as we have noted, there are many people, and even some powerful political groupings, in member states who question the whole principle of common developmental aims on which such policies are built. Some might even question the feasibility of addressing social exclusion issues in this way. Some put regional loyalties even above national allegiance, let alone any feeling of attachment to the idea of a European entity.

Europe's information society policies have been developed and to some extent implemented against a continuous and perhaps growing background of scepticism.

First steps towards a European information society

Whatever difficulties there may have been in formulating and managing effective policies at a European level, it is nevertheless the case that the people of the member states have enthusiastically embraced ICT. The Information Society Index (ISI) provides a useful indicator of Europe's position in global terms.[17] ISI divides countries into 'skaters', 'striders', 'sprinters' and 'strollers', using the following definitions:

- *Skaters* are 'in tune with . . . the information age . . . established infrastructure and computer literate population'.
- *Striders* are 'moving purposefully along the information pathway . . . absorbing new technologies...with a mixture of caution and conviction'.
- *Sprinters* are 'progressing in short bursts . . . needing to stop and shift priorities due to economic, social and political pressures'.
- *Strollers* are 'wandering towards the revolution . . . deterred by infrastructure costs, limited consumer demand and cultural fears'.

Countries are placed in a category determined by a score derived from a range of indicators, which include:

- *computing infrastructure* (PCs per capita, and some more complex measures of use by various subsets of the population)
- *information infrastructure* (access to telecommunications and broadcasting)
- *internet infrastructure* (number of users in various subsets of the population and e-commerce expenditure)
- *social infrastructure* (measures of press freedom, secondary and tertiary education and so on).

No such system can be ideal, but ISI provides a reasonably robust and objective measure drawing, for the most part, on reliable and verifiable data sets. The 55 countries that are listed in the Index account for 97% of global GDP and 99% of global expenditure on ICT.

On this basis, all EU member states are either 'skaters' or 'striders', but with a noticeable gap the northern and the southern states (Table 5.1). Indeed, there are significant differences between member states, in some of which there is still no formal development of information society policies at national level.[18]

Table 5.1   *EU member states in the ISI index*

Country	World ranking
Sweden	1
Finland	3
Denmark	5
Netherlands	7
United Kingdom	12
Germany	13
Belgium	*15*
Austria	*16*
Ireland	*19*
France	*21*
Italy	*23*
Spain	*24*
Portugal	*26*
Greece	*29*

Key: Skaters in **bold**; striders in *italic*.

Source: ISI; see note 17. No statistics are available for Luxembourg.

Of the potential member states, the Czech Republic and Hungary are striders (placed at 27 and 28 respectively between Portugal and Greece), but Poland (30) is a stroller.[19] The other skaters include two European countries which have chosen not to join the European Union (Norway (4) and Switzerland (8)), two in Asia (Japan (10) and Singapore (11)), and three others (USA (2), Canada (6) and Australia (9)).

Europe's road to an inclusive information society

The Delors Report (1993)

In 1993, under the Presidency of Jacques Delors, the European Commission published a 'white paper' (a policy proposal to the Council of Ministers) entitled *Growth, competitiveness and employment: the challenges and ways forward into the 21st century.*[20] This proposed a new programme to replace and subsume the existing information society projects that had been funded under FP4, including ESPRIT and the Telematics Applications programmes. The genesis of this strategy can be traced back to a number of green and white papers published on telecommunications issues in the middle to late 1980s. Telecommunications policy, and in particular the deregulation of the existing national monopolies, had played an important catalysing role in the Commission's desire to foster an information society in Europe.[21] However, the well-defined but complex information society strategy and policies that the EU and member states developed during the second half of the 1990s owes much to the 1993 White Paper, which came to be known as the Delors Report. It was accepted by the Council of Ministers meeting in Brussels on 5 December 1993.

The Delors Report's main aim was to stimulate a detailed and wide-ranging debate on developing the European economy in the 21st century; Delors envisaged a Europe that would be unified, flexible in its desire to adapt, and sustainable:

> We are faced with the immense responsibility, while remaining faithful to the ideals which have come to characterize and represent Europe, of finding a new synthesis of the aims pursued by society (work as a factor of social integration, equality of opportunity) and the requirements of the economy (competitiveness and job creation).

The aspiration to develop a 'new synthesis' and 'our wish to take our place in this new world' were to be reflected and repeated *ad nauseam* in the subsequent developments that arose out of this document. The Commission began to use the phrase 'information society' as a catchall to represent its view that there was a 'new industrial revolution', which itself reflected a new global society that had quickly adapted to and developed ICT as part of its everyday life.

As we suggested in Chapter 1, there are strong arguments against regarding the 'information society' as being one solely based on developments in ICT.[22] We have suggested that there is a number of reasons for such caution, not least the potential for ICT to perpetuate existing inequalities and even to create new social and economic divisions. Moreover, it is possible to regard ICT as simply the latest stage in a linear progression of communication media developed over many centuries; on that view, ICT is a new technology but not necessarily the precursor or progenitor of a new world. As we shall see, the Commission has been influenced by this perspective, and has tried to ensure that the information society is not simply a measurement of ICT penetration in the Union.

The Delors Report itself represented the first major step in the evolution of the European information society programmes, and ultimately aimed to develop a community of European nations that could compete effectively with Japan and the USA. In addition to developing an 'effective' information society, notably by encouraging the deregulation of telecommunication services in the Union, the Report also prioritized development of 'equitable' services, which would benefit everyone. From the beginning of this explicit policy of promoting an information society, therefore, there were two significant strands: to create a society that was effective and efficient, while also creating one that was equitable and inclusive.

The basic action plan for developing the information society contained in the Delors Report was based on five priorities:

- promoting the use of information technologies through the funding of project work between member states, and the promotion of flexible work models such as teleworking
- providing basic trans-European services for broadband telecommunications
- providing a regulatory framework for the information society, including strengthening legislation on intellectual property and data protection
- developing education and training to enable everyone to benefit from the information society
- improving industrial and technological performance through

research and development that would make industry more competitive.

The Report proposed the establishment of a Task Force on European Information Infrastructures, which would develop a report on specific priorities for the information society. This was established under the chairmanship of Martin Bangemann, the Vice-President of the Commission. The final version of his report, entitled *Europe and the global information society*, was ready for the meeting of the Council of Ministers in June 1994.[23]

The Bangemann Report (1994)

The Bangemann Report, as it came to be known, was presented to the Council of Ministers at its meeting in Corfu in June 1994. The Council considered that it provided a solid rationale for developing an information society policy. Its proposals were adopted in a decision that marked the start of the implementation of the European Union's information society policy.[24] Subsequently, the Bangemann Report provided an effective basis for further development of EU policy in this field.

The Report included a number of recommendations on how the EU could best move towards an inclusive information society. The cornerstone was to be a liberalization of telecommunications policy to achieve universal access to networks. Like Delors, Bangemann was not content to make suggestions without reference to the apparent 'newness' of the information society, and he too emphasized the need for urgent action: 'Throughout the world, information and communications technologies are generating a new industrial revolution already as significant and far reaching as those of the past.'

But this was more than mere repetition of what Delors had already said, and more than simply a further rehearsal of the benefits of ICT. Bangemann offered a range of positive reasons to embrace this 'revolution', which would 'create an information society'. These included 'the creation of a more caring European society' and the development of a wider choice of services and entertainment, and of 'new products and services'. Bangemann also opened up a vision of a European Union and member state governments which would be able to provide 'more efficient, transparent and responsive public services'. The prime mover for developing this information society was to be the private sector; the revolution was to be financed not by national governments or by the Commission, but by efficient public–private partnerships. In Bangemann's vision, government at both European and national levels would provide the strategic framework, and the policy, legislation and 'cohesion' of the information society. Private enterprise would build the new infrastructure and provide the services and products for this new society. The past, a time before the 'information revolution', was to be left behind with its 'monopolistic and anti-competitive environments'. Truly, this was to be a revolution delivering a new, attractive, prosperous, educated and inclusive information society. In fact, the truly new element was the European dimension, and the attempt to spread the benefits of the information society across all the member states. It was in this Union-wide dimension that Bangemann was most innovative and had the greatest potential to drive change.[25]

Europe's way to the information society: an action plan (1994)

The adoption of the Bangemann Report by the European Council in June 1994 was followed in July by the publication of another Commission document entitled *Europe's way to the information society: an action plan*.[26] The Action Plan addressed various areas of interest that had been identified in the Bangemann report, and offered a range of follow-up measures to implement them. The publication of this plan, and the subsequent adoption by the Commission of methods to measure, catalogue and promote the information society in the 1990s and beyond, marks the beginning of a distinctive phase of European policy.

The Commission's decision in 1993 to try to steer the evolution of the information society came at a time when the 'information revolution' was itself entering a phase of rapid development. It coincided most notably with the growth of the world wide web and digital mobile telephony.[27] Some member states, such as Denmark and Finland, took their own decisive actions in 1994 with visions and strategies for implementing information society policies in their own countries. Within three years of the adoption of the Action Plan, most member states had taken their first steps towards developing information society policies based either on EU strategy or on generic national strategies for incorporating ICT into society as a whole. In many ways, 1994 can be argued to mark the beginning of the information society concept and strategy in the European Union. Since that time strategies have been developed at European and national levels to try to address the speed of change and the need to adapt.

The Commission took a four-fold approach in the action plan to develop an information society strategy. It identified:

- the need to develop and update *the regulatory and legal framework* concerning ICT. In particular, there was a heavy emphasis on liberalizing the telecommunications regimes in Europe and opening up the remaining state-run monopolies to competition. In some countries (such as Finland) this was not difficult, while in others (such as Greece) it was to give real problems to the Commission. Elsewhere, the Commission identified other legal problems stemming from digitization, notably intellectual property, data protection and data privacy issues.
- the need to stimulate developments regarding efficient *telecommunications networks*, both terrestrial and satellite, and the desirability of providing basic services on these networks. While the Commission made it clear that the 'private sector' would be 'entrusted' with creating the networks, funding was to be made available by the Commission for pilot studies. Realizing the scope of this task, the Commission offered to act as a 'facilitator' for public and private organizations who were interested in 'partnership-building'.
- the need to ensure *economic, social and cultural benefits for society as a whole* from the uptake of ICT. Of the four main aspects of Commission policy, 'societal aspects' was the most difficult in terms of developing measures of success. While later action plans were to specify benchmarks for society's uptake of ICT, *Europe's way to the information society* confined itself to proposing a so-called High Level Group of Experts to investigate the issues involved. This body was duly established in 1995, and published a number of reports to which we shall return.[28]

- the need to *promote the information society*, by means of 'information days' and 'multimedia demonstrations'. Additionally, dissemination of material would use 'all methods of electronic publishing and information distribution'. Later in 1994, the Information Society Project Office (ISPO) was set up to provide the focus for this information dissemination and promotion.[29]

This Action Plan remains the basis of the Commission's information society policies, although it has been regularly revised since 1994. The first major revision was in November 1996 with the adoption of *Europe at the forefront of the information society*, often known as the 'rolling action plan' because it takes account of the changing priorities that the Commission had had to adopt and deal with since 1994.[30] The 1996 revision took more account of the 'people first' arguments raised by the Information Society Forum and others, against the seeming over-reliance on technological development and competition issues contained in the original action plan.[31] Further revisions in 1996 and 1999 retained the same basic structure and outlook, while shifting the emphasis to reflect political and social change. Liberalization of telecommunications, life-long education and retraining, specific programmes to develop ICT, benchmarking and publicizing examples of best practice have all featured continuously in the Commission's plans since 1996.

Implementing the information society in Europe

The Delors Report, the Bangemann Report and the 1994 Action Plan attempted to provide a framework for the orderly development of an information society in the European Union. The Commission had, in effect, identified the great social and economic changes that were taking place, and focused on technological change (especially in ICT developments) as their principal cause. They sought to harness and exploit these changes for the benefit of Europe as a whole by liberalizing regulatory frameworks and creating a climate in which initiative and entrepreneurship were encouraged. This was, in part, to be facilitated by pump-priming through funded projects, as well as by continued monitoring of developments by groups of experts. In global terms, the Commission's initiative was argued to be bold and innovative. In the early 1990s, few countries had gone beyond the point at which the development of networks was being encouraged. This was certainly the position, for example, in the USA, where the 'information superhighway' concept was effectively being left to the private sector, although in the context of a very liberal regulatory regime. In most European states, by contrast, little or nothing was being done to encourage such developments. The European initiatives were intended to be decisive in developing the infrastructure for an information society.

The High-Level Expert Group, of 14 'renowned' experts was set up in May 1995, following the 1994 Action Plan. Its remit was to advise the Commission on strategy. The Group published a number of reports, most notably *Building a European Information Society for us all* in 1996.[32] A crucial passage in this document expressed a concern about the technological focus of the Delors–Bangemann strategy. The Group argued that greater emphasis should be placed on the integration of people and organizations into the information society, to balance the emphasis on the technological, economic and industrial aspects. It argued further that the main focus of the EU information society strategy should be on the development of a knowledge-based 'learning' society, and 'not just an information society'. The Group had, in effect, recognized that technology alone was not enough, and that ICT merely provided a powerful range of tools. It looked more deeply into how these tools might be used, and indeed at why they should be used at all. The technological determinism that had silently informed the development of Europe's information society policy up to this point was not entirely abandoned, but it was criticized and was to be very significantly modified.

Perhaps the Group's most important conclusion was that the technological focus of the EU's policy was actually discouraging public support for the measures that were being implemented or proposed. Basing its argument on the idea that imposing technological change on society without first changing social and organizational cultures was flawed, the Group concluded that the technological–determinist model of growth would not work. Therefore, the Group argued, the policy would stand little chance of success if people felt disenfranchised by it, or were simply ignorant of the need for change. In its

Final Policy report, published in April 1997, the Group identified ten 'challenges' that EU strategy and policy should address:

- knowledge and skills acquisition
- the role of public services
- the emerging value chain
- scope for decentralization and the implications for work organization
- time management
- globalization, and its effects on employment and capital flows
- social exclusion
- bridging geographical distance
- European diversity
- enhanced democracy, and the potential of ICT to make it more 'transparent'.

Many of these key issues were incorporated into the plans for the Union's Fifth Framework Programme (FP5) to run from 1998 to 2002.[33] FP5 recognized the major importance of the information society, and the largest single tranche of funding was allocated to the theme of developing a user-friendly information society. Funding could be sought for research into four major areas:

- *systems and services for the citizen,* including projects on education, health, transport and the environment
- *electronic trade and new methods of work,* including not only e-commerce, but also social issues such as individual privacy and data protection
- *multimedia and electronic publishing*
- *essential technologies and infrastructures.*

In practice, this was implemented in a number of the key areas that had already been identified in the 1994 Action Plan, although with an approach in which social issues were to the fore. We shall consider each of these in turn.

Liberalization of telecommunications regimes

This was high on the EU's agenda even before the Delors Report, and was one of the central pillars of the Delors and Bangemann proposals, and of the 1994 Action Plan. It was adopted by the Expert Group as an essential precondition for all the other things that they wished to do, as well as being a political necessity. The underlying principle was to increase competition in the telecommunications sector, while making it easier for consumers to benefit from the results of competition by getting cheaper and better services. The overall objective was to encourage the use of networks. Ironically, by the time FP5 was formulated, this long-standing issue was probably of lesser significance than at any time in the previous decade. Technological change, and the commercial developments that followed from it, had made network access easier than ever before, and offered virtually seamless access to all networks because of the rapid developments in communications software. The rapid development of the use of mobile telephony overtook some of the problems that the EU had intended to address. The Commission had set up a Forum in December 1996 to discuss the future of mobile telephony. By February 1997, it was claiming to be leading negotiations 'from the front' in its dealings with the World Trade Organization (WTO) which was developing an Agreement on Basic Telecom Services.[34] WTO, like the EU was trying to set rules for service providers, to liberalize telecommunications services and to lever 'very significant' price reductions.

Regional strategy

The EU's regional strategy for the information society had originally been based on developing businesses and their supporting infrastructure in Europe's regions, and particularly on promoting new business opportunities based on ICT in less favoured regions. A conference held in December 1997, to promote cohesion between 'regions in the information society', marked the first move towards a 'regional' information society strategy. The conference considered financial incentives given to information society projects as part of EU structural funds and the various roles that might be played by national governments and by telecommunications operators.[35] This partly reflected the continuing perception among some in the Commission that the liberalization of telecommunications regimes was the panacea for the problems besetting European industry. But other issues were emerging. It was recognized that member states were moving at very different speeds in promoting ICT, a fact reflected in the ISI data that underlies Table 5.1.[36] It was clearly essential to counteract the creation of a two-speed Union, at least in respect of these crucial infrastructural issues.

Again, action began before the adoption of FP5 and was subsequently absorbed into it. The Commission had launched two projects in 1995 and 1997 to improve cohesion. First, it released funding for information society pilot projects under the European Regional Development Fund (ERDF) and the European Social Fund (ESF). Secondly, the Commission supported the creation of the Regional Information Society Initiative (RISI) in 1995, a joint project between its Directorate-General V (Social Affairs) and Directorate-General XIII (Telecommunications and Information Market). In 1997, it added the associated Inter-Regional Information Society Initiative (IRISI).[37] Both programmes were intended to foster co-operation between European regions, and to develop best-practice strategies for developing an information society and thereby promoting economic regeneration.

After the RISI and IRISI programmes came to an end in 1998, the European Regional Information Society Association (ERISA) was formed to take forward their work. It described its task thus:

> The information society is a dynamic concept. As the IRISI initiatives have demonstrated, it is likely to take different forms in different contexts depending on the structure of local productive systems, local institutions, and the demand expressed by the population. For these reasons, the Commission has no ready-made solutions; it does, however, have a methodology to propose and the instruments to accompany it. The point of departure is the recognition that the regional level is the most appropriate for identifying the opportunities offered to it by the information society. Only an approach based on consensus, partnership and dialogue among users and ICT providers within the regional context can make the information society a reality adapted to the needs of people and firms rather than a celebration of technology.[38]

The 28 regions that had developed their own information society strategies founded ERISA; the number of members had risen to 34 by the end of 2000. As with RISI and IRISI, the ERISA programme aims to identify and develop best practice, share knowledge and promote the recognition that the regional level is appropriate level for developing information society strategies.

Education policies

The development of effective teaching and learning strategies within the information society is critical to its development; indeed it could be argued to be as important as the ICT infrastructure itself. Without adequate teaching and learning of basic digital skills, ICT remains in the hands of the information-rich, and opportunities for both employment and social enrichment are lost. The well-publicized problem of the shortage of suitably qualified people to work in the sector supports this view.[39] Education has been supported by a number of strategies and initiatives, notably under the FP5 User-friendly Information Society action, which offered funding to relevant projects, and the Telematics Application Programme which had a specific action line to support Telematics for Teacher Training.[40] More recently, the Commission's adoption of the eLearning Action Plan in March 2001 presented a new impetus for ICT education and training for the information society.[41]

The eLearning Action Plan consists of four priority actions, all to be achieved by 2004, and all very ambitious in the light of uneven development across the member states:

- *improving infrastructure and equipment*, with internet access to be available from all classrooms by 2002, and a ratio of 1 PC to every 5–15 students by 2004
- *ICT training opportunities for all*, with all students leaving school 'digitally literate' by 2003, and educators themselves to be appropriately reskilled to facilitate this
- *developing 'quality content and services'* to support learning
- *networking of all schools* in the member states.

Working within the same time frame and providing a complementary vision to that set out in the *eEurope: an information society for all*,[42] the eLearning Action Plan represents a major step forward in the Commission's drive to foster an information society in Europe.

The Bangemann Challenge

In January 1995, the City of Stockholm initiated a biennial competition for cities in Europe to encourage the development of ICT-based services. The prize was to be awarded to the city that provided the best information services to its citizens, taking into account the extent to which those services benefited the whole community. The competition was named the Bangemann Challenge, to honour the Commission Vice-President who had done so much to promote the information society concept within the Union. The main goal of the Bangemann Challenge was to encourage cities to integrate ICT and promote best practice in the EU. In January 1997, however, it was opened up to cities throughout the world, thus reflecting the desire of the Commission to develop the information society at a 'global level'. When Bangemann himself left his post in the Commission in 1999, the competition was renamed the 'Stockholm Challenge' from 2000.[43]

The Challenge has proved to be a welcome one. There were 741 entrants in 2001, with projects into the following categories:

* new economy
* education
* health and quality of life
* public services and democracy
* culture and entertainment
* environment
* a global village.

The Stockholm Challenge programme is both a statement of Europe's commitment to its own information society, and a recognition of the global dimension of the issues that this raises. The level of response is in itself a demonstration of its relevance.

Moving forwards: the eEurope Action Plan

Between 1994 and 1999 the EU's information society strategy and the actions taken by member states became numerous and well reported, but they were also sometimes confusing and even overwhelming in their scope. In addition to all the reports devoted to aspects of information society development and the various action lines, the need to benchmark and to measure the reality of the development of the information society become increasingly important. This is amply demonstrated in the work done by the European Survey of Information Society Projects and Actions (ESIS) in providing an inventory of information society projects carried out in the EU and other European countries in the late 1990s.[44] Without benchmarking in a society increasingly reliant upon ICT for work, communication and leisure, the problems of formulating relevant and realistic policies would obviously be even more difficult.

Models of best practice were also needed for development of the information society. In the late 1990s, there was, as we have seen, a significant rethinking of some of the core issues and this led to consideration of such matters as sustainability and long-term social effects of the use of ICT.[45] This was part of a broader agenda driven by the Commission's desire to present a better image, and to promote the European institutions as less remote and bureaucratic. Romano Prodi, who succeeded Delors as President of the Commission, exemplified this in a speech to the European Parliament in February 2000 in which he pledged to change the way in which the Commission worked:

> I am committed to closing the gap between rhetoric and reality in Europe. People want a Europe that can deliver the goods. The Commission is committed to deliver . . . we will review our priorities and focus on our core business.[46]

Inevitably, not all the critics were satisfied. Indeed it has been argued that despite the gradual changes of approach since 1994, the information society initiatives are actually creating unemployment because of the kind of economic growth that they stimulate, and that the principles of the 1994 Action Plan are not sustainable in the longer term.[47]

This desire for change, and to 'deliver the goods', is reflected in the eEurope initiative[48] (otherwise known as *eEurope: an information society for all*) programme, which set a range of targets and identified the priority areas for developing the information society in Europe. For the first time in the EU's information society strategy since 1993, a range of specific actions with measurable outcomes was identified. Launched on 8 December 1999, and endorsed by the Council of Ministers in June 2000, the results of the initiative will be measured in 2002. In terms of presentation, the initiative presents straightforward objectives, and a range of clear actions. The three prime objectives are:

- *access to the internet* for all EU citizens, homes and businesses
- *digital literacy* for all EU citizens as an outcome of the related e-learning programme[49]
- *social inclusion* as a characteristic of the information society.

The achievement of the third objective is essentially dependent on the achievement of the first two. The emphasis on social inclusion as the long-term objective, however, is a significant change. The impact of ICT is now seen as much more than technological or economic as was the case in the mid-1990s. The heavy emphasis on telecommunications policies is, in any case, no longer necessary, since the changes have been largely achieved, although even newer technologies are continuing to have an impact, as we shall see. At the same time, ICT is now seen as more than the merely economic tool envisioned by Delors; employment is no longer the only driver.[50]

To realize these objectives, the initiative proposed ten 'priority areas' for further action. These actions revisit areas that have been well-trodden in earlier EU strategies:

- 'European youth into the digital age'
- cheap internet access
- fast internet access
- encouraging e-commerce
- smart cards for electronic access
- risk capital for 'hi-tech' small- and medium-sized enterprises (SMEs)

- participation for the disabled
- health online
- intelligent transport
- government online.

Some of these targets are clearly reiterations of existing objectives under a broader umbrella. 'European youth into the digital age', for example, refers to the objective of that strand of the eLearning programme that is designed to provide internet access for all schools by 2002. Some reflect new technological developments, particularly in mobile telephony. As we saw in Chapter 2, 3G mobile telephony promises fast access to the internet.[51] However, the telecommunications companies that successfully bid for 3G licences need to recoup money invested in spectrum auctions. Indeed, the objectives of fast access and cheap access may well be in conflict, and the financial difficulties that beset some parts of the mobile phone industry in 2001 suggest that development may not be as smooth or as immediate as some have predicted. Moreover, not all the issues relating to network provision are yet resolved; the Commission has published proposals to 'unbundle' the local copper-axial loops by the end of 2001.[52] All of this demonstrates that the social, technical and commercial issues cannot be entirely separated. The EU is now trying a new approach, driven by social rather than purely technical or economic considerations, but this does not mean that it has necessarily yet found a comprehensive solution to the problems or a quick route to their solution.

This difficulty is further emphasized in some other strands of the eEurope programme. The need for risk capital to support SMEs in the hi-tech sector became only too obvious towards the end of 2000, when stock markets began to turn against ICT companies. This included not only the so-called 'dot.com' enterprises, which were new and typically under-capitalized, but also the well-established global telecommunications companies, which experienced their own difficulties at the same time. Encouragement for e-commerce will be needed for some time to come. The Commission's approach has been to legislate to ensure a level playing field for organizations involved in digital commerce, notably in the fields of data protection[53] and copyright. But the promotion of smart card technology addresses another emerging issue of e-commerce – consumer suspicion and resistance. The promotion of smart-card technologies will be a key element in maximizing the potential benefits of e-commerce for both suppliers and customers.

It is in the social and political arena that the eEurope plan is most innovative and arguably at its most ambitious. Developments of ICT support for transport and health, for example, have been sporadic and disparate. They are now to be systematized. Similarly, the use of ICT to help disabled people, as well as other socially and economically disadvantaged groups, is a new initiative at this level. Finally, the governments of member states are encouraged to provide more information through their websites and databases, exemplified by the redesign and relaunch of the UK government website in February 2001.[54]

European organizations and institutions

It is in the nature of the European Union to create institutions and organizations to take its policies forward. In 1994, in meeting one of the strategic goals of the Action Plan, the Commission created the *Information Society Promotion Office* (ISPO) as part of the *Information Society Activity Centre* (ISAC). This was to be managed jointly by Directorate-General III (Industry) and Directorate-General XIII (Telecommunications and Information Market), a reflection of how this policy was perceived at the time. D-G XIII was actually renamed the Information Society Directorate-General, as a reflection of the importance attached to the information society by the Commission.[55] It was primarily designed to 'guide' the general public and to provide them with information about the 'tools' and 'choices' available to them in the new information society. Although its work was targeted at citizens in general, there was a particular emphasis on those in public administration and SMEs, and others who could benefit directly from new services, a new telecommunications regime, and similar changes. ISPO was also designed to develop and maintain various inventory projects. It became the European arm of the Global Inventory Project (GIP)[56] agreed at the G8 meeting in 1995, and was responsible for initiating Europe's first inventory programme, the European Survey of

Information Society (ESIS) initiated early in 1997.[57] ISPO's outputs include the ISPO website, which is intended to act as a starting point for those interested in the European information society.[58] Between June 1996 and June 1999 ISPO produced an informative and sadly missed *Information Society News* newsletter, which provided monthly and bimonthly updates on ISPO's activities and overall EU strategy.

The Information Society Forum, a 'think tank' created by the Commission in 1995, comprises 128 members intended to represent a cross-section of European industry, politics and society. The Forum has six working groups, each of which produces an annual report on its activities. These deal with impact on the economy and employment; social and democratic values; influence on public services; education, learning and training in the information society; the cultural dimension and the future of the media; and sustainable development, technology and infrastructure. The Forum's annual reports present a wide range of opinions on the information society, and have tended to reflect a slightly sceptical and somewhat politicized reading of the challenges faced in Europe. Notably, concerns have been expressed about the potential for an intrusive 'snooping society', and the need to protect individuals from invasions of their privacy. Elsewhere, doubts were raised on the social exclusion that ICT developments could potentially create, and fears were expressed about the dangers to citizen's rights in the so-called 'age of telework'. The Forum has acted as a sounding board for the Commission, with advice given on the overall strategy and success of the various information society programmes.[59] It is in this context that we should consider one final aspect of EU information society policy: how to measure its achievements.

Measuring the information society in Europe

The desire to measure and catalogue the development of the information society, difficult as it is, has been evident from an early stage in the evolution of the EU's strategy.[60] As we shall see later, the desire to measure progress in the information society by means of benchmarks is now a key component of the Commission's eEurope initiative, which was set in place in 1999.[61] As long ago as February 1995, at a G8 Information Society conference, the Commission and the Japanese government initiated the Global Inventory Project.[62] This was designed, as the title might suggest, to catalogue, and provide a repository for, all information society projects carried out in the EU and Japan. GIP aimed, to disseminate examples, through the internet, of best practice and to 'foster international alliances' in future information society projects.

GIP has been followed by other examples of information society measurement in the EU, notably ESIS.[63] ESIS began as a two-year project in 1997, but proved to be so successful and useful that it was renewed in 1999, as ESIS-II, for a further two years. For ESIS-II, the geographical scope of the project was extended, so that it included not only the member states of the EU, but also the countries of central and eastern Europe, and of the Mediterranean littoral. The data that it collects includes measures such as access to telecommunications and the internet, ownership of home computers, televisions, and mobile telephones, and other key measures of access to systems and networks. ESIS also records and analyses the projects funded by the EU in its various information society and information technology programmes. The data provide invaluable insights into some aspects of the progress made in Europe in the 1990s.[64] A mere 430 projects were recorded in 1994; by 1998–2000 this had risen to over 1,800. Even more significant, perhaps, was that the effect of the modifications to the Delors–Bangemann approach were beginning to make themselves felt. While only 15% of the projects were concerned with infrastructure and 19% with technological development work, 57% dealt with applications; of these nearly half were in the field of education and training. The statistics also reveal some failures to achieve targets; less than a quarter of the input into the projects comes from the private sector, with the rest coming from various government agencies, international organizations and the EU itself.

In defining benchmarks for measuring the progress of the information society, and in collecting and publishing relevant data, the European Union has sent an example to the rest of the world. Its initiatives, both within its own boundaries, and with other partners in G8, have influenced UNESCO in establishing its information society barometer website, which provides information on virtually all information society initiatives around the world.[65]

Conclusion

This brief and much simplified survey of the European Union's collective attempt to promote the development of an information society in western Europe has highlighted some the issues that are being generated by the perception that an information society is a desirable and attainable objective of public policy. The specifics are, of course, a product of the unique nature of the European Union itself. The generic issues, however, are relevant to all advanced societies, and to those countries that aspire to advanced status. These include:

- maintaining a balance between technological change and social developments
- defining the respective roles of the public and private sectors
- ensuring that benefits reach into all parts of society and all geographical regions
- encouraging the development of new modes of commerce and new methods of work.

All of these issues are as global as the information society itself. They are being addressed at every level from small local communities to international organizations. Governments are being forced to redefine their own role, and their relationships with their citizens and with the commercial world, from SMEs to multinational corporations. Emphases vary. We might have considered Singapore, for example, where government has played a key role both in developing a very sophisticated technological infrastructure and in controlling its use.[66] Public libraries have played a key role in the strategy, and there are close links with education at all levels.[67] We might have looked at the USA, where the private sector reigns supreme, and issues of social inclusion are arguably not being addressed as they are in Europe. The solutions that are adopted to the problems of the information society will be as diverse as the political and cultural traditions of the countries and regions in which they arise.[68] In our final chapter, we shall try to pull together some of these themes as we consider the uncertainties of the future.

A note on further reading

This chapter covers many complex policy issues in the context of an exceptionally complicated organization and its institutions. For current material on the EU, the only readily accessible source is the Europa website (note 1), but this is always 'under construction' and despite a recent revamping is still very difficult to use (see below, p. 171). Even so, EU documents are more easily found here than in hard copy in libraries. Intelligent use of the ISPO parts of the site (note 29) can be particularly helpful. Once again, however, intelligent reading of newspapers is essential. For specific topics, a search of the Europa website, followed by searches of the web archives of newspapers (see below, p. 172) is probably the best initial approach.

Notes and references

1   Those unfamiliar with the complexities of the European Union's institutions and structures will find a helpful brief introduction on its own website at
    http://www.europa.eu.int/inst_en.htm
    In what follows, we shall assume that the reader is aware of the respective roles of such bodies as the Commission, the Council of Ministers and the Parliament.

2   Commission of the European Communities, *Communication from the Commission to the Council, the European Parliament, the Economic and Social Committee and the Committee of the Regions: the Commission's work programme for 2000*, CEC, 9 February 2000 (COM (2000) 155 final), 6.

3   The six original members were Belgium, France, Germany, Italy, Luxembourg and the Netherlands. Denmark, Ireland and the UK joined in 1973, followed by Greece (1981), Portugal and Spain (1986), and Austria, Finland and Sweden (1995). Norway's attempt to join in 1973 was rejected by a national referendum. Further expansion is envisaged; the candidate countries include the Czech Republic, Poland, Hungary and Slovenia, and the three Baltic republics (Estonia, Latvia, Lithuania). For the historical background, see
    http://www.europa.eu.int/abc/history/index_en.htm
    For a broader and objective historical perspective on the devel-

opment of the Community, albeit dating from the late 1980s, see Kennedy, *Rise and fall*, 608–31. A more sceptical view is implicit in the comments of Norman Davies, *Europe: a history*, Oxford University Press, 1996, 1126–7.

4 Partly in recognition of these tensions, we have tried to be careful to use the word 'Europe' *only* when we mean the geographical entity. We describe the 15-member community as the 'EU' or the 'Union'. No political view is intended to be conveyed by our use of this terminology.

5 See below, pp. 115–16.

6 See below, pp. 117, 122–3.

7 The Framework Programmes (FPs) are the umbrellas under which the EU's research and development agenda is progressed. The current programme is the Fifth (extending from 1999 to 2002), and puts a particular emphasis on the 'new economy' and on knowledge-led economic growth. For a presentation designed as an introduction to FP5, see **http://www.eu.int/en/comm/eurostat/research/summary/ tsld001.htm**

8 See above, pp. 69–70.

9 On the latter point, see H. Von Heilmcrone, The efforts of the European Union to harmonize copyright and the impact on freedom of information, *Libri*, **50** (1), 2000, 32–9.

10 *Growth, competitiveness, employment: the challenges and ways forward into the 21st century – White Paper*; 5 December 1993 (COM (93) 700) (known as the Delors Report).

11 *Europe and the global information society – recommendations to the European Council*. For the Bangemann Report, see below, pp. 108–9.

12 See above, pp. 11–14.

13 One short-term fix proposed by the UK is to relax immigration controls allowing ICT professionals from outside Europe to apply for jobs in the UK. See David Walker, Statistics show immigration beneficial to economy, *Guardian*, 29 January 2001, to be found at **http://www.guardian.co.uk/Archive/article/0,4273,4126367,00. html** See also above, p. 88, and note 16.

14 See above, pp. 18, 61–2.

15 See above, pp. 51–3 and 60–1.

16 On this point, see Nicholas Garnham, Europe and the global information society: the history of a troubled relationship, *Telematics and Informatics*, **14** (4), 1997, 323–7. Garnham argues that this motive is in conflict with the long-standing desire to develop a common European telecommunications regime, and that the tension will eventually destroy the whole information society strategy.

17 For this index see the ISI website at **http://www.worldpaper.com/ISI/**

18 See Nick Moore, Is the European information society working? A review of progress in the member states of the European Union, *Alexandria*, **11** (1), 1999, 39–50.

19 There are no statistics for the potential members in the Baltic.

20 See note 10, above.

21 On this point, see the paper by Garnham, cited in note 16.

22 See above, pp. 15–19.

23 The report can be found at **http://europa.eu.int/ISPO/docs/basics/docs/bangemann.pdf**

24 For an account of these and subsequent events, see the European Commission's Information Society website, history pages, at **http://europa.eu.int/ISPO/basics/i_history.html**

25 See, for example, the commentary in H. Kubicek, Information society or information economy: a critical analysis of German information society politics, *Telematics and Informatics*, **13** (2–3), 1996, 165–75. Kubicek argues that Germany had been moving in this direction for 30 years, and that Bangemann added nothing to the German agenda. This is true, but it misses the point.

26 *Europe's way to the information society: an action plan*, 19 July 1994 (COM 347 (94) final).

27 See above, pp. 36–7.

28 See below, pp. 112–3.

29 For ISPO, see **http://www.europa.eu.int/ISPO/**

30 *Europe at the forefront of the global information society: rolling action plan*, 31 July 1997 (COM (96) 607 final).

31 For the Information Society Forum, see below, p. 122.

32 *Building the European information society for us all: final policy*

report of the high-level expert group, April 1997.

33 For the Framework Programmes, see above, p. 98 and note 7.

34 *Information Society News*, February 1997.

35 [Editorial in] *Information Society News*, March 1998, 1.

36 See above, p. 105.

37 Information on RISI and IRISI can be found on the ERISA website. A range of material is available on the programmes. See **http://www.erisa.be/**

38 *Cohesion and the information society*, 22 January 1997 (COM (97) 7 final).

39 See above, p. 102.

40 *Learning in the information society: action plan for a European education initiative (1996–98)*, Communication to the European Parliament, the Council, the Economic and Social Committee and the Committee of the Regions. See **http://europa.eu.int/comm/education/planht.html**

41 Commission of the European Communities, *The eLearning Action Plan: designing tomorrrow's education*, CEC, 28 March 2001 (COM (2001) 172 final).

42 For which, see below, pp. 119–21.

43 The Stockholm Challenge website contains a range of information on the Challenge, its background and past winners. See **http://www.challenge.stockholm.se/challenge.html**

44 For an account of ESIS, see **http://www.europa.eu.int/ISPO/intcoop/esis.html** See also below, p. 123 and note 63.

45 The Information Society Forum's Working Group 4 has published a number of annual reports considering globalization and sustainable development. See **http://members.tripod.com/ruddyconsult/expo2.htm**

46 *Prodi, 2000–2005: shaping the new Europe*, Speech to the European Parliament, 15 February 2001. See **http://europa.eu.int/comm/external_relations/news/ 01_00/doc_00_4.htm**

47 See SophiaKaitatzi-Whitlock, 'Redundant information society' for the European Union?, *Telematics and Informatics,* **17** (1), 2000, 39–75.

48 A substantial range of material on the eEurope initiative is pub-

lished on the ISPO website at **http://europa.eu.int/ISPO/**

49 For which, see above, pp. 116–17.

50 See above, pp. 112–13.

51 See above, pp. 37–8.

52 Commission of the European Communities, *Communication from the Commission to the Council, the European Parliament, the Economic and Social Committee and Committee of the Regions. The introduction of third generation mobile communications in the European Union: state of play and the way forward*, CEC, 20 March 2001 (COM (2001) 141 final).

53 Directive 95/46/EC of the European Parliament and of the Council of 24 October 1995 on the protection of individuals with regard to the processing of personal data and on the free movement of such data. *Official Journal L 281*, 23/11/1995, 0031–0050.

54 The new site is
    http://www.ukonline.gov.uk

55 The Information Society Directorate-General's website provides information on their roles and responsibilities. See
    http://europa.eu.int/comm/dgs/information_society/ mission_en.htm

56 See below, p. 123.

57 See below, p. 123.

58 At **http://www.europa.eu.int/ISPO/flash.html**

59 A useful introduction to the ISF's work will be found in its first annual report at
    http://www.europa.eu.int/ISPO/policy/isf/documents/ rep-96/ISF-REPORT-96.html

60 For a general survey, see A. Ricci, Measuring the information society: dynamics of European data on usage of information and communication technologies in Europe since 1995, *Telematics and Informatics*, **17** (1–2), 2000, 141–67.

61 See above, pp. 119–21.

62 See **http://www.gip.int**
    For a complete listing of relevant G8 projects, see
    http://www.gip.int/g8/gip.htm

63 For an account of ESIS, see
    http://www.europa.eu.int/ISPO/intcoop/i_esis.html

See also Ana Maria Correia and Marie Alexandre Costa, European Survey of Information Society (ESIS): the Portuguese experience, *Journal of Information Science*, **25** (5), 1999, 381–93.

64 The most comprehensive set of data is at
 http://eu-esis.org/Basic/basic2000.htm

65 UNESCO's 'Observatory on the Information Society' provides an excellent resource for information society developments around the world. It has the additional merit of being logically designed and consequently easy to use. See
 http://www.unesco.org/webworld/observatory/index.html

66 See M.-J. Kim, A comparative analysis of the information sectors of South Korea, Singapore and Taiwan, *Information Processing and Management*, **32** (3), 1996, 357–71.

67 Julie S. Sabaratnam, Planning the library of the future: the Singapore experience, *IFLA Journal*, **23** (3), 1997, 197–202.

68 There is an interesting analysis in Chris Yapp, The knowledge society: the challenge of transition, *Business Information Review*, **17** (2), 2000, 59–65.

6

The future

Introduction

The scientist is engaged in the business of observing and explaining phenomena, whether these are physical, biological or social. For social scientists, the observation, evaluation and explanation of societal phenomena lies at the core of their discipline. Their analyses enable us to understand more about the society in which we live, and in which others live, and with the passage of time become the raw material of history. In Chapter 1, we considered the work of a number of social scientists (and others) who observed the development of a knowledge-based economy in the middle of the 20th century and tried to explain it. Some found that explanation in technological change, and developed a determinist model, which others firmly rejected. Some indeed emphasized continuities, and saw both social and technological change as now more than the latest point in a continuum that stretched over many centuries. This view is certainly sustainable.[1] All commentators agree, however, that *something* has happened and is continuing. Whether this is an evolutionary change in western society or a fundamental paradigm shift in human communication can be the subject of legitimate debate. The truth is, of course, far more complicated than that simple contrast implies. Our conclusions depend on which country we study, which socio-economic groups are the focus of our study, and our approach to the analysis of the process of the communication of information.

Our view is essentially pragmatic. Governments and supra-national bodies like the European Union perceive the existence of an information society and predict its continued development. By that alone, they effectively ensure that such a society is part of the political agenda and is a real phenomenon. In this final chapter, therefore, we shall try to explore some of the implications of the development of the information society for the future. We are not engaged in the business of predicting technological change. Futurology is an inexact science; for every Arthur C. Clarke who predicts global satellite communications a decade before any man-made object has left the earth's atmosphere, there are a dozen who have predicted two-hour flights from London to Sydney in the year 2000. There will continue to be advances in the technologies of communication and information. Biological computers and quantum computers cannot yet be built, but nor could the Turing Machine when Turing conceptualized it, less than a decade before ENIAC was operational.

If we accept past continuity, however, we can reasonably project some lines of future development, if only in the comparatively short term. We can, for example, assume continued investment of public and private funds in the development of fixed-line and mobile telecommunications networks, and the continuing convergence of formerly separate systems and technologies. We can assume the continued growth of the applications of information and communications technologies in business, government and education, as well as in the social and private lives of individuals. We can also assume a continuation of the gap between the most and least privileged, those with and without access to information and communications technologies and all that they can do.

Convergence and cross-over

The telecommunications network

The convergence of technologies is often seen as one of the key developments of the 1990s, but it deserves a little further analysis. The obvious examples lie in the use of telecommunications networks for a great variety of purposes. In 1980, the public telecommunications networks were used, in effect, only for voice communications; Telex was a rare exception to the rule, and it was never in general use outside large organizations and businesses. The developments of the next two decades transformed the way in which the networks were used, and indeed the networks themselves. Even in the field of voice communications, there were significant changes. The development of global systems, based on satellite transmission of digital signals, transformed international telecommunications. Direct dialling to anywhere in the world became possible in all the industrialized countries. Political considerations delayed the introduction of direct dial facilities in some countries, but even in many of them the pressure was so great from the international business community that some provision had to be made.

Some were excluded from this revolution, as they had been from what preceded it. It remains the case that 99% of the population of Africa have never initiated a telephone call, and that there are fewer telephones on that continent than there are in the Borough of Manhattan. For those with access, however, that access gives more than ever before.

The enrichment of voice communications is only one aspect of the transformation of the telecommunications networks, and arguably not the most important. Fax is best understood by remembering its rarely used full name – facsimile transmission. A document is digitized, transmitted through the telecommunications network and received in the form of an identical reconstruction of the original document by the receiving apparatus. Fax is now a daily tool of business and government, and increasingly in use by individuals for their own private purposes. Telex and telegrams have vanished from most industrialized countries because fax is a far more efficient means of doing what they could do and much more besides. Signatures, for example, can be transmitted by fax, and are accepted for many transactions.

The changes in telecommunications are symbolized by the domestic telephone. In 1980, it was precisely that, a telephone. It could be used to initiate and receive calls, and for nothing else. In the year 2000, a typical instrument can be used for voice communications, to send and receive faxes, is linked to an answering machine or a voice-mail box, and probably doubles as the domestic photocopier as well. Its touch-tone 'dialling' system allows the user to go through a menu of options offered by the computer that answers calls in many large organizations. Meanwhile, many of the household's voice calls are made and received on a mobile phone, which also has a voice-mail box and can be used for sending and receiving text messages, and has, of course, the full range of touch-tone facilities. Soon it will have fax and e-mail facilities as well. A pager completes the current suite of personal communications devices, but there are more to come.

When we look beyond the instrument to the network, the change is even more profound. The transmission of digitized data is now the primary preoccupation of network providers. The physical rebuilding of networks across the industrialized world has provided the capacity to send millions of bytes of data across countries and continents using land lines and microwave transmissions via satellites. The internet has both piggybacked on this and forced its further development. The domestic telephone connection, a simple mono-dimensional piece of technology only 20 years ago, is now the slip road to the information superhighway.

The domestic PC, which facilitates personal use of the internet, is only the present stage of development and already the outlines of the future are becoming clear. The PC itself is a multipurpose machine. It can stand alone as a word processor, as a multimedia CD player or as a platform for games. It can be at either end of a communication chain through an ISP using the public telecommunications networks, and through the same channels it can transmit and receive faxes. The PC is already close to being a single centre of domestic entertainment, communication and information. Its competitor is a new generation of televisions, which differ both in hardware and in network facilities from their familiar predecessors. Like domestic telephony, domestic television was transformed in the last two decades of the 20th century.

The changes began in the USA with the development of cable television in the late 1970s. Cable was not a new phenomenon. It was familiar in some parts of the USA from the 1950s onwards as an attempt to overcome the inadequacies of broadcast transmissions. Cable rediffusion was used in areas where reception was poor.[2] Cable was seen as an essentially local phenomenon, rather than a significant medium. Only in the mid-1970s did this change, with the development of cable-specific channels, beginning with Home Box Office, the first of the pay-to-view movie channels. Others followed for movies, sport and a multitude of special interests. Although cable remained an American phenomenon until the 1990s, it was important in creating the first truly multi-channel access to television.

The next phase of change was the development of satellite television. Although satellite has developed in the USA (and indeed provides part of the network for the cable companies), it is essentially a European and (increasingly) Asian phenomenon. It was introduced into Britain in 1989 by two rival providers, British Satellite Broadcasting (BSB), owned by a consortium of terrestrial television companies, and Sky Television owned by Rupert Murdoch's News International Corporation.[3] Satellite broadcasting brought the multichannel culture to Europe, and brought with it a new variety of access to television. In Asia, it brought, for the first time, easy access to western television, not least to western news programmes such as CNN and BBC News 24, with a significant impact on politics in the Philippines, Indonesia and elsewhere.

The satellite broadcasters, however, do not confine themselves to broadcasting. The digital systems and receivers that became available at the end of the 1990s are interactive. Perhaps the most familiar aspect of this is the gimmick of interactivity in the live broadcasting of sporting events. The viewer can switch between different camera angles, follow a particular player or see an analysis of the game. But interactive television is not just a gimmick. Sky now offers e-mail facilities; interactive shopping is surely on the horizon, a logical development from the existing shopping channels. The set itself has other capabilities. It can, of course, be the platform for the viewing of videotapes. On the horizon, however, are more radical developments. With its stereo sound system, it could be linked to an audio CD player, or to a PC with DVD facilities. Convergence has remade the television, just as it has remade the telephone. Moreover, it has made them into competitors for much of the same ground. E-mail by television and downloaded movies through an ISP and a telephone line exemplify the crossover.

Convergence of technologies and the creation of new competitive arenas are one measure of change. Essentially, this whole process is driven by consumer demand, even if that demand has to be created by making technologies available. Perhaps the best example of this is the mobile telephone. In much of the industrialized world, mobile phone use is now commonplace.[4] Ubiquity came quickly in the wake of the construction of reliable and universal cellular networks. Within a very short space of time in the later 1990s, mobile phones could be used as a link between a portable computer (laptop or smaller) and the internet. The next generation of phones, using WAP technology, provides direct access to the internet. There are still problems to be solved and the first examples of WAP phones are distinctly user-unfriendly, but the message for the future is clear. The mobile phone network providers will also become ISPs, just as the satellite broadcasters have done. The challenge is not only to fixed line telephones or to the telecommunications networks that link them; it is to the supremacy of the PC itself as the means of access to digital communications whether by voice, data or fax.

Print or electronic format?

The convergence of technologies is creating an overlap of function for content as well as for hardware and media. In particular, ICT poses a significant challenge to the historic western dependence on the printed word. Since the early 1990s, many traditional reference books have been re-engineered in electronic formats. Some of these take the form of CD-ROMs, while others are accessible online; some indeed are available in both formats, depending on users' need for completely current information and their ability to pay for it. For many people throughout the industrialized world, the use of a web search engine is now the normal starting point for discovering information. This presents its own problems. The search engines do not engage in qualitative selection analogous to that which underlies the development of the stock of a library. Their comprehensiveness – which in one sense is one of their greatest benefits to the user – has the disadvantage of producing huge lists of possible references even on comparatively specialized or minor topics. The information seeker of the first decade of the 21st century has had to develop new skills in differentiating between the accurate and the inaccurate, the good, the bad, the foolish and the simply meretricious.

Some may regret the shift from print to electronic formats, but regret is pointless because the shift is irreversible. The issue that now confronts us is to change our approach to education so that users have the skills to benefit from the technologies to which they have access. This means far more than mastering the simple skills of using a PC and the barely more complex skills of searching the web. It means developing the intellectual and analytical skills to enable the searcher to form a valid judgement about the material that the search reveals. Far from simplifying the learning process, or 'dumbing down' to use a favourite phrase of some British observers, the use of ICT has made it more complicated and more sophisticated. It has also increased its potential. Learners are no longer restricted to the materials that their place of learning can provide. Indeed, the whole concept of a 'place of learning' may be becoming outmoded in itself, although the social aspect of school and college should not be underestimated, and we shall return to it.

Books, of course, are for entertainment as well as instruction. The 'replacement' of books by electronic media raises the emotional temperature, especially among some older people. There are two issues that need to be distinguished: the use of electronic media as a substitute for books, and the alleged diminishing popularity of leisure reading under the impact of new forms of entertainment, most of them audiovisual and many of them electronic. We will deal first with second point, and then return to the question of electronic 'books'.

It is a matter of historical fact that during the 20th century, when new media from cinema to DVD competed for leisure time and leisure spending, the number of books produced and read increased at a rate without precedent in history. The rate of increase far exceeded the rate of population growth or the rate of increase in literacy. Indeed, each of the new media in turn created its own demand for printed books.[5]

All this, it should be remembered, took place against a background of an ever-widening range of leisure activities and ever-increasing competition for leisure expenditure. The market is the essential determinant of success and failure. The development of electronic books is a good current example of the issues involved. Electronic journals have been familiar in the academic world for a number of years, and their use is now widespread. Major publishing houses, such as Elsevier, now see this as a profitable market.[6] Indeed, electronic journals are now established as part of the common currency of academic and professional communication, especially in disseminating the results of primary research. On the whole, electronic publishing has so far proved to be a less satisfactory mechanism for leisure reading, exemplified by the recent experience of the science fiction writer, Stephen King. In July 2000, King began to publish his latest novel, *The Plant*, on his own website.[7] The scheme involved relying on the honesty of readers to pay for the materials they accessed. If enough people paid, King would then mount the second part, and in due course the third, and so on. Eventually, six parts were published in this way. King himself considers the experiment to have been a success,[8] although some journalists did not entirely share this perception.[9] The figures on King's own website show a total income of US$720,000, yielding a profit of US$465,000 for an author whose revenues would normally be measured in millions.[10] Nevertheless, the more perceptive publishers recognize that King's experiment has serious potential to change the nature of their profession by effectively eliminating them as middlemen.[11]

The innovative part of King's experiment was not online publication of fiction *per se*; it was the method of payment. More typically, payment is by access, as it is for scientific journals. The British novelist Frederick Forsyth is only one of many authors who have published work online, to which access is by prior payment by credit card.[12] Forsyth and King are perhaps the best-known authors to venture into online publication, but an increasing number of books is available. It is important to recognize, however, how the authors and distributors expect the books to be used. The assumption is that the reader will download the text and print it for reading.[13] Only very recently have manufacturers begun to make available hand-held devices for reading continuous text, which bear some resemblance to a book and have some of the convenience (such as being small and lightweight) that is associated with printed books.

Convergence of media and content

Convergence is often presented as if it were a purely technological issue. There is, of course, an important technological dimension to it. The fundamental factor is that digital data can be transmitted, stored and retrieved without regard for its content or its form of output. Whether the data will be retrieved as text, sound, images or all three is irrelevant. The essential point is that the data is digitized for storage and transmission. It is this that has facilitated convergence, and has made our computers into entertainment centres, and our televisions into computers. Convergence, however, goes further than technology. We can see also a convergence of media and content, less easily defined but in some ways even more powerful in its implications. Consumers have an ever-increasing range of choice about how to access the information or entertainment which they want. The choice is, to some extent, constrained by availability; some of the constraints are artificial, and are designed to protect intellectual property rights or other forms of investment. A well-known recent example is the legal proceedings against the producers of the Napster software that allowed free distribution and downloading of music on the internet. The music industry saw the potential for the loss of hundreds of millions of dollars, and successfully intervened to have the facility withdrawn. Ironically, one consequence was an alliance between Napster and Bertelsmann, the German-based multinational media corporation, to develop the service in a more formal way.[14] Meanwhile, it was reported in April 2001 that some 37 million Americans were regularly downloading music from the internet.[15] It is clear that the battle is far from over.

The Napster affair, in which a piece of software was developed by a student and made freely available on the internet,[16] is a forceful example of the changes that are flowing so rapidly throughout the industrialized countries. In late 2000 and early 2001, Bertelsmann was not the only company to take a more realistic view of Napster than those who were trying to put it out of action. Here was a commercial opportunity, for if there is one certainty that has come out of the affair, it is that the demand for downloading music is huge, and the ability to do so is uncontrollably widespread. Napster challenges the economics of the music industry at its most vulnerable point – the protection of its intellectual property. It raises questions about whether current intellectual property regimes are sustainable at all in the age of universal digital communications. It illustrates the power of the combination of communications networks, digital technologies and cheap hardware. It illustrates that the impact of convergence is only just beginning.

Napster has vividly exposed the radical changes that are taking place in the information marketplace. Convergence is creating crossover. Consumer choice is no longer confined to which of a handful of television channels to watch. It includes whether to use the television as a platform for videos or computer games, or as a means of access to the internet for business or pleasure. It includes whether to find information in a book or on a website. It includes whether to make a phone call, or send a text message or an e-mail from anywhere in the world where there is a digital network for mobile telephony. Competition is placing power in the hands of the consumers; convergence and cross-over exemplify that power.

The consequences of change

Change has winners as well as losers. Technological development leaves some people in its wake, downgrades occupations and may even destroy a whole way of life. In the middle decades of the 19th century, for example, the infrastructure and services that had developed around road and canal transport all but vanished in the face of the advancing rail network. In the late 20th century, the railroads in the USA and shipping lines everywhere, went into near-terminal decline in the face of competition from cheap air travel. In the history of communications we can see similar cycles of change. Printing replaced handwriting for many purposes from the middle of the 15th century onwards. In the second half of the 20th century, telephone calls took the place of personal letters in much of the industrialized world. From the 1960s onwards, newspaper circulation fell dramatically in the face of competition from television; so did cinema attendance and many other activities. By the end of the century, fax had replaced telex and telegrams, and e-mail was challenging the role of the telephone, the written message and even face-to-face conversations in many people's lives.

Such changes happen unevenly. All of those we have mentioned had their first impact on existing elites who were wealthy enough to travel, sufficiently well educated to be literate or with the means to buy leisure activities or communications equipment. But their effects spread more widely than that. The mere existence of the technologies and their products creates a market.[17] In the second half of the 19th century, cheap and easy rail travel created holiday resorts and indeed the whole concept of the regular holidays for the mass of employed people. The pattern was repeated in the late 20th century when jet travel brought formerly unimaginable destinations within reach of millions. Printed books made it easier to learn to read, and indeed to do many other things. Modern information and communications systems have made it easier to find out about everything, and cheaper and easier to communicate. New varieties of ICT – from the pocket calculator in the 1970s to the WAP phone and portable electronic book of the new century – have started as gadgets, and after a brief spell as fashion accessories have become (or will become) part of the norm of daily life.

The issue, however, is more than one of early or late adoption of new technologies. Late adoption, or non-adoption, is not always a matter of choice. It may be imposed by a political decision. In the former Soviet Union, for example, the technology to provide international direct dialling was available long before it was accessible. Delayed adoption may, however, be a consequence of social and economic deprivation, and inability to buy, understand or use the technology. Sub-Saharan Africa painfully illustrates the point. For a variety of reasons – which include economic weakness, political incompetence and low levels of education – telecommunications infrastructures are so poorly developed over much of the region that participation in internet-based activities is almost impossible. Even voice communications and fax are still difficult, especially domestically, in some countries. The various measures of access and use have profound implications.[18] It is not simply that the majority of the people in these countries are 'information poor'; they are fundamentally unable to remedy this.[19] There is a whole bundle of issues that can barely be disentangled and that have to be addressed systematically. Telecommunications infrastructures are an essential part of a modern economy, but without them such an economy can be neither created nor sustained. Only in a comparatively prosperous economy can universal education be provided at a reasonable level, and indeed it is only in a comparatively prosperous society that the majority of people can allow their children to take advantage of it even when it is provided without charge. Only in an educated society, however, can the majority of people take advantage of the opportunities that communications create. Can the vicious circle become virtuous? To some extent, technology can address the problems it has partly created. Mobile telephony, for example, may preclude the need to develop extensive and expensive fixed line networks in difficult terrain and sparsely populated territories in the developing countries. The solutions however are long-term, and the problems are now.

We should not, however, make the mistake of assuming that the gaps are only between the industrialized and less developed parts of the world. The increasing prominence of the social agenda in the European Union's information society policies is a recognition that such gaps exist even in the wealthiest countries.[20] The pace of change is leaving little room for making mistakes. It is already the case that those who lack all IT skills are disadvantaged in many ways. Within a very few years they will be in the same position as the person living in a remote rural area with no car, and perhaps unable to drive, when the bus services are withdrawn because the minority they serve no longer make them profitable.

Creating change

The policies that are being developed in the European Union illustrate how some of the issues can be addressed. We have suggested that these include not only the social consequences of technological change, but also such matters as the relationships between the public and the private sectors, and the development of new economic structures that take advantage of the power of ICT.[21] In other words, more changes can be created if the process can be managed.

The business world

In the business world, we can already see some of that change happening. The well-publicized failures of some dot.com companies should not blind us to the fact that e-commerce is here to stay. Even many of those who have sustained personal losses from company failures recognize the long-term potential.[22] A combination of lack of capital, poor marketing and weak management may have destroyed many of the dot.coms, but not before it had become clear that there is a market for the services that they can offer if an economic way can be found of reaching it. Even some of the most spectacular 'failures', in terms of the value of their shares, are still trading.[23] Large companies are adopting e-commerce with alacrity, and much of what has been predicted for a decade or more is becoming a reality. It is now possible, for example, to shop for food and other goods on a supermarket chain's website and, as a registered user, pay by credit card and have the goods delivered. In the travel industry, the use of the internet is becoming normal for individuals as well as for travel agents, whether for travel bookings, hotel reservations, car hire or indeed entire holiday packages. Internet banking is on the increase despite public doubts about security issues. The web has become a virtual high street.

Electronic access to conventional businesses merges almost imperceptibly into genuine e-commerce, where the product or service can only be accessed or ordered electronically. On the other hand, successful e-commerce has many of the needs of traditional business. Banking illustrates this. Access to banking facilities through the web is not difficult to establish; indeed it is probably more difficult to persuade customers of the security of the transactions. The online banks are typically closely associated with existing financial service providers, which have the skills and the capital needed for the enterprise to succeed.[24] This is not to deny that internet banking is innovative, and well suited to the needs of many customers; indeed, the fact that other banks have followed down the same road demonstrates that demand is there. The two great benefits of e-commerce are the customer's convenience (most obviously in 24-hour access), and cost savings, which can reduce prices and increase profits.

It is not only in the business world that change is being created for the benefit of providers and consumers alike. Professional services are being transformed in the network environment.[25] Legal and medical advice are both available online. In the UK the NHS Direct online service, although it is still far from perfect in either content or searchability, is widely used as a first point of consultation for those with concerns about their health. No profession is unaffected by this and similar developments.[26]

Education and training

Education and training are also undergoing great change. Within schools and colleges, ICT is to be found in the classroom and lecture theatre, as well as in libraries and other learning resource centres. It is used to support student learning, and to test the acquisition of learning. Computer Aided Learning (CAL) and Computer Assisted Assessment (CAA), although far from universal, are widely used to supplement traditional face-to-face contacts with teachers and interactions with fellow students. The material is typically delivered across a network, often with a familiar web-like interface. Although some is confined to institutional intranets, in principle it can of course be made universally available, with or without charges for access.

The most remarkable example to date has been the decision by Massachusetts Institute of Technology to make all its courseware freely available on the web, as a means of 'widening access to education and inspiring others to participate'.[27] This is very different from the commercial virtual universities that are beginning to have some impact on the educational scene in North America, such as the University of Phoenix, where 'you just click into a class and start learning'.[28] The British Open University is also making increasing use of CAL, both on disk and networked, and many universities around the world are looking to network delivered distance learning as an important element in their future strategies. The Higher Education Funding Council for England is leading the development of an e-university as a collaborative activity between a number of existing institutions.[29] There are scores of similar initiatives in the USA and Australia.

Innovative approaches to the provision of professional services and of education raise many questions about the quality of the provision, and even of legal liability for the advice provided. The best of them are authoritative referral or support services, which help the client to deal with a professional in due course and perhaps provide either online contact with a professional or give a telephone number through which help can be obtained. There may be a danger of professionals becoming more remote from their clients; the optimistic view is that clients will become more knowledgeable, more discriminating and more challenging, and thus force professionals into offering even higher quality of service. There is some evidence to support this view,[30] although it is also clear that not all professionals entirely welcome these developments.[31]

The use of ICT to promote and conduct business, and to support learning and to deliver professional services, illustrates the range and depth of its penetration into the way of life of many people in the developed countries. It also, however, emphasizes the danger of exacerbating existing social and economic divisions within those countries. The public provision of network access has not developed as quickly as the networked services that are available. The European Union's information society policies neatly illustrate the need for a twin-track approach: on the one hand, use of the network is encouraged, and on the other there is support for network development and provision, and for training in its effective use.

In practice, much of this is actually delivered at national or regional level. In the UK, for example, we can see a whole cluster of policies that are promoting the development and use of electronic networks. Public access is largely to be achieved through public libraries, all of which will have broad bandwidth connection to the internet by 2005.[32] This initiative, called The People's Network, does not, however, stand alone. Lifelong learning, an essential element in responding to economic and social change, is being promoted through many initiatives, including the University for Industry, whose Learn Direct system gives access to learning packages at all post-compulsory levels for any learner. Delivery will largely be through specially established learning centres, but Learn Direct itself can be accessed from any networked workstation.[33] The learning packages that are offered include training in the use of ICT, while for those with no skills, and perhaps no network access, most local further education colleges now offer regular and heavily subscribed courses in basic IT skills. Many initiatives are also being mirrored at regional and local level, with the development of access points in community centres, shops, and even in public houses in some parts of the country. Content is often supported by local government authorities, and there are facilities for voluntary organizations to provide their own content through an organization called Beehive, which provides templates for website development and offers free server space to community organizations.[34] Similar developments can be found throughout Europe.

The implications of change

From supranational bodies to village football teams, organizations are making themselves known through the world wide web, a system that was familiar to only a handful of specialists just a decade ago but which is now all but synonymous with the internet itself for most people. A whole new industry has grown up around the web, with consultants, site designers, hosts and search engines. There are few organizations or activities that do not have a web presence. This is often described as anarchic, although in fact it is well-organized and strictly controlled. The registration of a URL, the *sine qua non* of a website, is carefully regulated. The search engines are, for the most part, professionally managed, and systematically search the web continuously for new sites, which are then classified and indexed. The ISPs exercise a degree of control over what sites can be accessed through their servers. There is a steady increase in the patrolling of the web by those who seek to enforce existing laws and develop new forms of content control.

Although there is regulation, the web nevertheless represents the largest public space in human history. Indeed, it might be thought to have restored some of the characteristics of public space that Habermas argued had been lost in the high tide of the domination of the mass media in the second half of the 20th century.[35] Among the millions of websites there are hundreds of thousands owned by individuals or small organizations or interest groups, which could never have hoped to reach a wider public through conventional means such as publication or broadcasting. On the web, however, not only do they achieve a public presence, they achieve it globally. There is, of course, a negative side to this. At its worst, the web is a facilitator of law-breaking. It can be used as a means for the distribution of child pornography, for inciting racial hatred or for promoting violence or even murder.[36] Quite apart from the direct consequence of such use of the web, the indirect effect is to lend support to those who call for closer regulation of web content through a system analogous to the classification of movies and videos. In practice, it is the ISPs who try to prevent access to such sites.[37]

The benefits, however, far outweigh the disadvantages, however distressing these may be to some people. At the highest level, governments and other powerful organizations can no longer hide. Of course, they control the contents of their own websites, and can and do use them for propaganda. But they have found that in practice the best use of the web is to make information available to the public.

Through the web far more official data is easily available than ever before, and official documents are far more readily accessible than they were when they could be found only in libraries and often after a long and complicated search. It is almost impossible for an organization to hide on the web. A search for McDonald's, for example, reveals not only the company's own website, financial data, and a great deal of promotional material, but also sites with names like *I Hate McDonald's*, *What's Wrong with Ronald McDonald* and *McSpotlight*, all of which are distinctly unfavourable to the company in tone and content.[38] A similar search for Railtrack, Britain's beleaguered railway infrastructure company, gives access not only to timetables, press releases and dozens of official documents, but also a site called *The Railtrack Scandal* containing statements that few newspapers would take the risk of publishing. The web has become a place for the expression of opinions and the conduct of debates that would be all but impossible in any other public space, and certainly not in any medium through which there was access to such a large potential audience.

The web is perhaps the most dramatic manifestation of the re-engineering of the use of public space for information and opinion in the industrialized countries. But there are others. The development of multi-channel television, delivered through satellite and cable, and increasingly with a community-based element is another. On the back of the highly profitable sport and movie channels it is possible, in theory at least, for the broadcasters to provide special interest channels, which attract perhaps only a few hundred viewers at any one time. As we have already suggested, the convergence of broadcasting and digital interactivity is going to lie at the heart of radical developments in the next few years.

Theory and practice

It is clear that the 'information society' is not a simple concept nor a single entity. There is force in the argument that all societies have always been dependent on knowledge and information, and that those that have been most successful are those that have developed means for storing and transmitting what has been learned.[39] This is not simply a matter of developing information media, whether on baked clay tablets or magnetic disks. It involves developing processes for analysing and classifying information, for storing the media and the information in a retrievable form, and for ensuring that potential users have access. In turn this means that users must have appropriate knowledge and skills to retrieve and use information. All of these principles were as true in ancient Assyria as they are in 21st century California. The difference is, it is argued, one of scale rather than principle.

When we look at the 'information society' that emerged in the late 20th century, we are essentially looking at the changes wrought because of a series of inventions and innovations in communications. Each in turn, brought with it social and economic change. The telephone changed the way in which people did business and conducted their social relationships. The cinema changed social habits and created a new form of popular entertainment. The radio brought other new forms of entertainment to millions of people, as did television a generation later. They had a deleterious effect on some other activities, and yet they were also intellectual, cultural and social stimulants and liberators. The worlds of drama and music, once the preserve of a wealthy elite, were made accessible to millions of people who could not afford to visit a theatre or a concert hall, or perhaps felt a certain diffidence in doing so. Social barriers were swept away, and for perhaps 30 years from the mid-1950s to the mid-1980s the western world shared common experiences to an extent without parallel in history. Images – the assassination of President Kennedy, Neil Armstrong on the surface of the moon – became common to all. Public events became part of private life. Ironically, this was achieved at the expense of public activity. Soap operas were an obsession for millions, and the lives of both their characters and the actors who played them became grist for the mill of the popular press and of hundreds of thousands of conversations. Yet although watching television can be a shared experience, it is not a communal one; there is a profound difference between watching *Hamlet* (or for that matter a football match) with two other people and watching it with hundreds (or tens of thousands). Even the interpersonal communications of the mid-century were essentially private – the telephone call, the telegram, the telex message. The measure of the change wrought by the development of networked computing is that new *public* worlds have been created.

The fragmentation of broadcasting is only one example of this, giving greater consumer choice. The internet and in particular the web have, as we have suggested, wrought a far greater change. The web is the ultimate public space, and yet can be used for the most intimate purposes. It is the creation of government agencies and some of the largest corporations in the history of the world, and yet it is open to everyone to contribute as well as to receive. Its underlying technology is the product of some of the most complex science and mathematics known to human kind, and yet it is so simple that anyone can learn to use it in a matter of minutes. This was the technological basis of the 'information society' that developed at the very end of the 20th century.

Are we then forced to agree with the technological determinists, those who argue that social and economic change have been driven by technology? Clearly, technological change has had a profound effect. But technologies are only adopted by societies that need them or can find a reason for using them. ICT has tapped into a vast unmet and perhaps largely unidentified desire for greater access to information, for greater understanding of the world around us, and for more control over the events that mould our lives. Cause and effect are almost impossible to distinguish. Governments have become more accountable, and more accountability is expected by those whom they rule. Which came first? We want more information about our health, and are no longer reliant on a few doctors to whom we have personal access to tell us about it. Did we always want to know more, or do we ask more questions because we can find the answers? Are we less deferential towards doctors and lawyers (and professors) because their knowledge is no longer a mystery, but is open to the whole world?

All of this poses new problems, and restates old one. As we become more accustomed to the idea of free access to information, how can the laws that protect intellectual property survive? New conventions are already developing. The Napster affair illustrated how one of the world's largest industries could come close to destabilization; only a multi-million dollar lawsuit was able to a stop a clever student from blowing up the music industry,[40] and even then only because some of the players effectively changed sides. They recognized that the technology was unstoppable. The web itself is based on software that was made freely available by Berners-Lee and others, partly from genuinely altruistic motives and a belief that the results of science should be accessible, but partly in some cases because of the perception that control was impossible. How long will conventional scientific journals survive? And what will be the consequences of payment by access and the inevitable limitations on browsing and serendipity?

Governments and supranational bodies like the European Union have only a limited control over all of this. The forward-looking element of the EU's information society policies, despite the criticisms that can be levelled at some aspects of them, is precisely that they recognize that the genie cannot be put back into the lamp. The policies are designed to exploit the ICT revolution for the benefit of as many people as possible. New regimes for intellectual property, data protection, personal privacy, freedom of information and pornography – huge as these issues are – are simply the spin-off from that simple recognition of economic necessity. The challenge is to ensure that the benefits outweigh the disadvantages, and that enough people understand enough of the issues to ensure that the benefits themselves can be defined.

Notes and references

1   Indeed, it is the thrust of the argument in John Feather, *The information society: a study of continuity and change,* 3rd edn, Library Association Publishing, 2000.
2   Winston, *Media, technology and society,* 306–11.
3   For an inevitably biased, but always lively and perceptive, view of the early years of British satellite television, see Andrew Neil, *Full disclosure,* Pan, 1997, 354–86.
4   Ironically, the major exception is the most telephone-oriented of all countries, the USA, as a consequence of regulatory restrictions.
5   Feather, *History,* 222.
6   See the company's website at
    http://www.elseviersciencedirect.com/
    for details of some of its services and publications. There are, of course, a number of other companies involved in the production of scientific journals online, but Elsevier can stand as an example.

7 http://www.stephenking.com

8 Stephen King, King's ransom, *Guardian*, 10 January 2001, G2, 4.

9 See, for example Jonathan Lambeth, King of horror fails to cast net wider, *Daily Telegraph*, 21 September 2000, dotcomtelegraph, 1.

10 The accounts can be found at
http://www.stephenking.com/PlantNumbers_010101.html

11 See the comments in Jason Epstein, *Book business: publishing past present and future*, Norton, 2001, 33–4. Epstein is one of the elder statesmen of American publishing (creator of Anchor Books, founder of the *New York Review of Books*, editorial director of Random House), but he is by no means a dinosaur.

12 See his collection of short stories, *Quintet*, of which the first was published in November 2000, available at
http://www.onlineoriginals.com/Quintet.html
Each of the stories costs £1.99 (US$2.99).

13 On King's website, for example, many of the FAQs revolve around difficulties encountered in downloading and, especially, printing.

14 Napster signs deal with Bertelsmann. 31 October 2000, in Guardian Unlimited Archives at
http://www.guardian.co.uk/Archive/Article/0,4273,4084305,00. html

15 See D. Ian Hopper, Study: 37 M Americans download music; Associated Press report at
http://dailynews.yahoo.com/h/ap/200110424/tc/ internet_music_2.html

16 For the origin of Napster, see Nick Paton Walsh, 'Mom, I blew up the music industry', *Observer*, 21 May 2000, at
http://www.guardian.co.uk/Archive/Article/0,4273,4020371,00. html

17 The whole of Winston, *Media, technology and society*, illustrates the point.

18 See above, pp. 60–1 for various data and comments on these matters.

19 Haywood, *Information rich*, offers a good analysis of consequences, but does not deal with the issue of remedies.

20 See above, pp. 112–13, 119–20.

21 See above, p. 124.

22 For an interesting analysis by a journalist turned dot.com businessman, see Andrew Marshall, Dot coma, *Independent*, 25 April 2001, Business Review, 1–2.

23 Most obviously, perhaps *lastminute.com* at
   http://www.lastminute.com

24 For example, the pioneering UK online bank, Egg, is associated with the long-established Prudential. See
   http://www.egg.com/visitor/.

25 See Richard Susskind, The impact of technology [on the professions], *RSA Journal*, 4/1, 2001, 21–2.

26 The site is
   http://www.nhsdirect.nhs.uk/

27 The words are those of Charles M. Vest, President of MIT, in announcing the scheme; see
   http://www.mit.edu/newsoffice/nr/2001.ocw.html

28 This institution offers programmes at various learning centres in the USA, but basically operates online; see
   http://online.phoenix.edu

29 See the press release at
   http://www.hefce.ac.uk/Pubs/CircLets/2000/cl04_00.html

30 Chris Swinson, Quality assurance, *RSA Journal*, 4/1, 2001, 23–4.

31 See the comments of Sir Christopher Paine, Doctors: society's whipping boys, *RSA Journal*, 4/1, 2001, 25–7.

32 For the original proposal, see Library and Information Commission, *New Library: the people's network*, published in 1997, and available at
   http://www.lic.gov.uk/publications/policyreports/newlibrary/index.html
   For progress and plans see
   http://www.peoplesnetwork.gov.uk

33 See **http://www.learndirect.co.uk**

34 The Beehive Network ironically has no home page of its own. The term 'Beehive Community Network' will produce a listing of local sites through all the major search engines.

35 See above, pp. 15–16.

36 We choose not to give URLs for such sites, some of which it is illegal to access in the UK and many other countries. But there

have been recent widely publicized examples of all three, including an international child pornography ring broken by the police, websites that are used to plan demonstrations against experimentation on animals, neo-Nazi websites and, especially in the USA, the publication of lists of clinics at which it is alleged that abortions are performed.

37 See above, p. 62, for Yahoo!'s action against a site selling Nazi memorabilia. Yahoo!, AOL and other providers operate filtering systems that effectively allow access to certain sites by those who are (or claim to be) over 18.

38 Conducted on Yahoo! on 1 May 2001.

39 This is not to deny that some pre-literate societies were highly successful, or that oral transmission of information is not still of great importance even in societies with universal literacy. But there are limits to the quantity of information that can be stored without a system that is not dependent on human memory.

40 For the phrase 'blowing up the music industry', see above, note 16.

Some suggestions for further reading

This book is an introduction to its subject, and covers a wide range of topics. All of the scores of books, articles and websites cited in the notes and listed in the Bibliography contain valuable and interesting further information, interpretation and opinion. For the comparative beginner, however, at whom this book is specially aimed, there is a number of publications that provide useful critiques and analyses. Here we recommend some additional readings – both printed and online – that provide an overview of the multifaceted information society.

For those wishing to delve into the conceptual issues, the best exposition of the various arguments for and against the idea of the information society is contained in Frank Webster's excellent *Theories of the information society* (Routledge, 1995). Webster considers the information society from a variety of standpoints (including technological, economic and employment-related criteria for measurement), and provides a readable introduction to the theories of Habermas and Bell, among others. This is an essential text for those studying the information society; Webster accurately sums up the problems of defining the information society as being synonymous with any one development, whether in ICT, in terms of the labour market or more generally in terms of social change.

Two other books are equally interesting in their scope and argument. David Lyon's *The information society: issues and illusions* (Polity Press, 1988) and William Martin's *The global information society* (Aslib/Gower, 1988, 2nd edn 1995), provide analyses of the information society written before the mass uptake of the internet, mobile telephones, and satellite television in the late 1990s. Of the two, Lyon's readable critique of what he refers to as the 'so-called information society' considers the effects of technological advance on society and the effects of global networks; Martin's equally readable work is more concerned with ICT and the various information industries. Both books provide useful overviews, and coincidentally provide snapshots of the information society at particular points in its development.

Finally, every serious student must eventually read Manuel Castells' trilogy of *The rise of the network society* (Blackwell, 1996), *The power of identity* (Blackwell, 1997) and *End of millennium* (Blackwell, 1998). All three books are excellent in their own right, and all will provide good background reading for understanding the information society concept.

While the internet does host a range of material on the information society, it is in keeping with the variable quality of websites in general that some sites devoted to information society issues are rather disappointing or, in some cases, fiendishly difficult to navigate. During research for this book, particular problems in regard to poor design, defunct pages and crucial omissions were noted. One site that successfully combined all three of these irritants was the EU's ISPO site (**http://www.ispo.cec.be/**). Thankfully, in May 2001, the site was replaced by the new Europa site (**http://europa.eu.int/information_ society/**), and we must hope that this will be developed to provide a straightforward one-stop-shop for those interested in information society strategy and policies. It remains the case, however, that while much excellent material is available on the web in regard to the European information society, the methods of finding this material can sometimes owe more to luck than judgement.

Nevertheless, determined searching of the mass of material linked from ISPO (which is archived and is still accessible) does reveal some publications that the student will certainly find useful for more advanced study. In regard to development 'indicators' and strategy, we recommend two publications produced by ESIS (European Survey of Information Society Projects and Actions). *Public strategies for the information society in the member states of the European Union* and *Information society indicators in the member states of the European Union* are both available on PDF format at their website (**http://europa.eu.int/ ISPO/esis/default.htm**). They provide excellent overviews of recent IS developments in the European Union. In future, the location of all information society material on the Europa server, and the development of this resource, should adequately reflect the obvious importance attached by the EU to these developments.

Perhaps the most attractive and well-designed website concerning the global information society is the UNESCO Observatory (**http://www.unesco.org/webworld/observatory/**), which provides regular updates on strategy and policy around the world, together with statistics on ICT penetration and usage. It is straightforward to navigate, and is recommended as a starting point for those wishing to consider developments in global information society strategy and policy.

The fast pace of ICT development requires some form of current-awareness service to keep up with developments. Although current-awareness websites concerning ICT news are common, we recommend *wired.com* (**http://www.wired.com**), which provides an extensive range of articles and opinion on ICT development. It also offers an extensive archive of articles, and provides a free daily e-mail digest of stories. Another less frequent, but equally useful, source of ICT development reflecting more upon UK and European concerns is the *Guardian*'s Online supplement (published every Thursday, and also available on their website at **http://www.guardian.co.u**k). Indeed, most of the world's serious newspapers now have regular features of this kind, and for the student who wants to keep abreast of developments, there is no substitute for regular critical reading of such material.

Bibliography

This is a complete listing of the works cited in the notes and references. In addition, we have listed all the websites that we have cited, some of which also appear in this bibliography.

Aslib, *The Aslib guide to copyright*, Aslib, 1994.

Baldwin, T. F., McVoy, D. S. and Steinfeld, C., *Convergence: integrating media, information and communication*, Sage Publications, 1996.

Banisar, D., Freedom of information around the world
http://www.privacyinternational.org/issues/foia/foia-survey. html

Belkin, N., The cognitive viewpoint in information science, *Journal of Information Science*, **16**, 1990, 11–15.

Bell, D., *The coming of a post-industrial society: a venture in social forecasting*, Heinemann, 1974.

Bernal, J. D., *The social function of science*, Routledge, 1939.

Berners-Lee, T., *Weaving the web: the past, present and future of the world wide web*, Orion Business Books, 1999.

Bootstrap Institute, Biographical sketch [of] Douglas C. Englebart
http://www.bootstrap.org/dce-bio.htm

Borko, H., Information science: what is it?, *American Documentation*, **19** (1), 1968, 3–5.

Bottle, R. T., Information science. In Feather, J. and Sturges, P. (eds), *International encyclopaedia of information and library science*, Routledge, 1997.

Bradford, S. C., *Documentation*, Crosby Lockwood, 1948.

Briggs, A., *The BBC: the first fifty years*, Oxford University Press, 1988.

Brown, M., A matter of timing, *Guardian*, 25 September 2000, Media, 2–5.

Brown, R. D., The shifting freedoms of the press in the eighteenth century. In Amory, H. and Hall, D. D. (eds), *A history of the book in America. Volume I, The colonial book in the Atlantic world*, Cambridge University Press, 2000.

BT slips to three-year lows
http://news.zdnet.co.uk/story/0,,s2085171,00,html

Buckland, M. K., *Information and information systems*, Greenwood Press, 1991.

Buckland, M. K., Information as thing, *Journal of the American Association of Information Science*, **42** (5), 1991, 351–60.

Bush, V., As we may think, *Atlantic Monthly*, **176**, 1945, 101–8.

Bush, V., [Design for the Memex]
http://www.dynamicdiagrams.com/design/memex/model.htm

Butterly, T., Constraints in the development of the 'wired' economy in Africa
http://www.nua.ie/surveys/analysis/africa_analysis.html

Castells, M., *The rise of the network society*, Blackwell, 1996.

Castells, M., *The power of identity*, Blackwell, 1997.

Castells, M., *End of millennium*, Blackwell, 1998.

Cellular Online, [Statistics of mobile phone ownership and usage]
http://www.cellular.co.za.

Chatrie, I. and Wright, P., *Public strategies for the information society in the member states of the European Union: an ESIS report*, CEC, 2000.

Clanchy, M. T., *From memory to written record*, Edward Arnold, 1979.

Cole, C., Shannon revisited, *Journal of the American Society of Information Science*, **44** (4), 1993, 204–11.

Collins softback English dictionary, 3rd edn, HarperCollins, 1991.

Commission of the European Communities, *Annual report of the Data Protection Working Party, 25 June 1997*
http://www.europa.eu.int/comm/internal_market/en/media/dataprot/wpdocs/wp3en.htm

Commission of the European Communities, *Building the European information society for us all: final policy report of the high-level expert group*, April 1997
http://www.europa.eu.int/ISPO/docs/topics/docs/hlge_final_en_97.doc

Commission of the European Communities, *Cohesion and the information society*, CEC, 22 January 1997 (COM (97) 7 final).

Commission of the European Communities, *Commission adopts the eLearning Action Plan* [Press release, 28 March 2001] **http://www.europa.eu.int/gettxt=gt&doc=IP/01/46**

Commission of the European Communities, *The Commission's work programme for 2000*, CEC, 9 February 2000 (COM (2000) 155 final).

Commission of the European Communities, *eEurope: an information society for all*, CEC, 8 December 1999 (COM (2000) 130 final).

Commission of the European Communities, *eEurope 2002: an information society for all. Draft action plan*, CEC, 24 May 2000 (COM (2000) 330 final).

Commission of the European Communities, *The eLearning Action Plan: designing tomorrow's education*, CEC, 28 March 2001 (COM (2001) 172 final).

Commission of the European Communities, *Europe and the global information society – recommendations to the European Council* **http://www.europa.eu.IASPO/docs/basic/I_history.html** [Bangemann Report].

Commission of the European Communities, *A European way for the information society: first annual report of the Information Society Forum*, **http://www.europa.eu.int/ISPO/policy/isf/documents/rep-99/ISFReport_en.pdf**

Commission of the European Communities, *Europe at the forefront of the global information society: rolling action plan*, CEC, 31 July 1997 (COM (97) 607 final).

Commission of the European Communities, *Europe's way to the information society: an action plan*, CEC, 19 July 1994 (COM 347 (94) final).

Commission of the European Communities, *Growth, competitiveness, employment: the challenges and ways forward into the 21st century – white paper*, CEC, 5 December 1993 (COM (93) 700) [Delors Report].

Commission of the European Communities, *The introduction of third generation mobile communications in the European Union: state of play and the way forward*, CEC, 20 March 2001 (COM (2001) 141 final).

Commission of the European Communities, *Learning in the information society: action plan for a European educational initiative (1996–98)*

http://www.europa.eu.int/comm/education/elearning/
eplanen.pdf

Commission of the European Communities, [Legislation on data protection]
http://www.europa.eu.int/eur-lex/en/lif/data/2000.en_
300Y1114_01.html

Commission of the European Communities, [Legislation on the protection of classified information]
http://www.europa.eu.int/eur-lex/en/lif/dat/2000/
en_300D0823_01.html

Commission of the European Communities, *Strategies for jobs in the information society*, CEC, 4 February 2000 (COM (2000) 48 final).

Concise Oxford dictionary, 9th edn (CD-ROM), Oxford University Press, 1997.

Correia, A. M. and Costa, M. A., European Survey of Information Society (ESIS): the Portuguese experience, *Journal of Information Science*, **25** (5), 1999, 381–93.

Davies, J. E., *Data protection: a guide for library and information management*, Elsevier, 1984.

Davies, N., *Europe: a history*, Oxford University Press, 1996.

de Solla Price, D. J., *Big science, little science*, Columbia University Press, 1963.

Dept for Education, *The National Curriculum: England*, DfE, 1995.

Dept of Trade and Industry, *Consumers' access to their credit reference files under the Data Protection Act 1988*, DTI, 1999.

Dodson, S. and Barkham, P., Why the net is not invited to Sydney, *Guardian*, 14 September 2000, Online, 2–3.

Doman, J., Uphill and down dale: citizens, government and the public library. In Criddle, S., Dempsey, L. and Heseltine, R. (eds), *Information landscape for a learning society: networking and the future of libraries 3*, Library Association Publishing, 1999, 133–44.

Dordick, H. S. and Wang, G., *The information society: a retrospective view*, Sage, 1993.

Dryer, J. S. (ed.), *Breadth and depth in economics: Fritz Machlup – the man and his ideas*, D. C. Heath, 1978.

Duff, A. S., Daniel Bell's theory of the information society, *Journal of Information Science*, **24** (6), 1998, 373–94.

Eisenstein, E. L., *The printing press as an agent of change: communi-*

cations and cultural transformation in early–modern Europe, Cambridge University Press, 2 vols., 1979.

Epstein, J., *Book business: publishing past present and future*, Norton, 2001.

Everard, J., *Virtual states: the internet and the boundaries of the nation state*, Routledge, 2000.

Feather, J., *A history of British publishing*, Routledge, 1988.

Feather, J., *Publishing, piracy and politics: an historical study of copyright in Britain*, Mansell, 1994.

Feather, J., *The information society: a study of continuity and change*, 3rd edn, Library Association Publishing, 2000.

Feather, J. and Sturges, P. (eds), *International encyclopaedia of information and library science*, Routledge, 1997.

Federal Reserve System, *Consumer handbook to credit protection laws*, Governors of the Federal Reserve System, 1993.

Findlay, M., *The globalisation of crime: understanding transitional relationships in context*, Cambridge University Press, 1999.

Fisher, D., British film and video censorship and classification **http://www.terramedia.co.uk/themes/british_film_censorship. htm**

Fukuyama, F., The end of history, *The National Interest*, **16**, 1989, 3–18.

Fukuyama, F., *The end of history and the last man*, The Free Press, 1992.

Garfinkel, S. L., *Architects of the information society: thirty-five years of the Laboratory for Computer Science*, MIT Press, 1999.

Garnham, N., Europe and the global information society: the history of a troubled relationship, *Telematics and Informatics*, **14** (4), 1997, 323–7.

Giddens, A., *Social theory and modern sociology*, Polity Press, 1987.

Giddens, A., *The third way: the renewal of social democracy*, Polity Press, 1998.

Giddens, A., *Runaway world: how globalisation is reshaping our lives*, Profile Books, 1999.

Gilster, P., *The internet navigator*, John Wiley and Sons, 1993.

Ginsbury, J. C., A tale of two copyrights: literary property in revolutionary France and America, *Tulane Law Review*, **64**, 1990, 991–1031.

Goedegebuure, B. G., Celebrating FID's centennial – the Tokyo Resolution, *FID News Bulletin*, **44**, 1994, 115–17.

Graham, G., *The internet: a philosophical inquiry*, Routledge, 1999.

Gray, J. C., *National information policies: problems and progress*, Mansell, 1988.

Habermas, J., *The structural transformation of the public sphere* [*Strukturwandel der Öffenlichkeit*], Polity Press, 1989.

Halbert, D. J., *Intellectual property in the information age: the politics of expanding ownership rights*, Quorum Books, 1999.

Hayes, R. M., A simplified model for the infrastructure of national information economies. In *Proceedings of the NIT '92 conference, Hong Kong, 30 November–2 December 1992*, 1992.

Hays Code, The
  http://www.artsreformation.com/a001/hays-code.html

Haywood, T., *Info-rich, info-poor: access and exchange in the global information society*, Bowker-Saur, 1997.

Henry, P. H., Roscoe 'Fatty' Arbuckle, 1994
  http://www.halcyon.com/phenry/text/arbuckle.tex

Herman, E. S. and McChesney, R. W., *The global media: the new missionaries of global capitalism*, Cassell, 1997.

Hesse, C., Enlightenment epistemology and the laws of authorship in pre-revolutionary France, *Representations*, **30**, 1998, 109–37.

Hewitt, P., Social inclusion in the information society, *RSA Journal*, **2** (4), 1998, 97–101.

Hodges, A., *Alan Turing, the enigma*, Simon and Schuster, 1983.

Hopper, D. I., Study: 37 M Americans download music [Associated Press report]
  http://www.dailynews.yahoo.com/h/ap/200110424/tc/internet_music_2.html

Hutton, W., *The state we're in*, rev. edn, Vintage, 1996.

Hyman, A., *Charles Babbage: pioneer of the computer*, Oxford University Press, 1984.

Index on censorship
  http://www.indexoncensorship.org/ii/iiintro.html

Information Society Forum, *A European Way for the Information Society*, Information Society Forum Secretariat, 1999.
  http://www.ispo.cec.be/policy/isf/welcome.html

Information Society Project Office, *Information Society News: news roundup from the European Commission's Information Society Project Office*, July 1996–June 1999. (Editions were produced by ISPO between July 1996 and June 1999. They were initially published monthly, but publication became erratic during 1998 and 1999. The final edition (number 29) was produced in June 1999. Back issues are available from ISPO at the time of writing.)

Johns, A., *The nature of the book: print and knowledge in the making*, University of Chicago Press, 1998.

Kaitazi-Whitlock, S., 'Redundant information society' for the European Union?, *Telematics and Informatics*, **17** (1), 2000, 39–75.

Kaplan, B., *An unhurried view of copyright*, Columbia University Press, 1967.

Katz, R. L., *The information society: an international perspective*, Praeger, 1988.

Kennedy, P., *The rise and fall of the great powers: economic change and military conflict from 1500 to 1800*, Fontana, 1989.

Kennedy, P., *Preparing for the twenty-first century*, Fontana, 1994.

Kim, M.-J., A comparative analysis of the information sectors of South Korea, Singapore and Taiwan, *Information Processing and Management*, **32** (3), 1996, 357–71.

King, S., King's ransom, *Guardian*, 10 January 2001, G2, 4.

Kubicek, H., Information society or information economy: a critical analysis of German information society politics, *Telematics and Information*, **13** (2–3), 1996, 165–75.

Lambeth, J., King of horror fails to cast net wider, *Daily Telegraph*, 21 September 2000, dotcomtelegraph, 1.

Landes, D., *The wealth and poverty of nations: why some are so rich and some are so poor*, Abacus, 1998.

Lawley, E. L. and Summerhill, C., *Internet primer for information professionals*, Mecklermedia, 1993.

Levy, D. A. L., *Europe's digital revolution: broadcasting regulation, the European Union and the nation state*, Routledge, 1999.

Library and Information Commission, *New library: the people's network* **http://www.lic.gov.uk/publications/policyreports/newlibrary/index.html**

Locke, J., *Two treatises of government*, Awnsham Churchill, 1690.

Locke, J., *Some thoughts concerning education*, A. and J. Churchill, 1693.

Lyon, D., *The information society: issues and illusions*, Polity Press, 1988.

McChesney, R. W., *Telecommunications, mass media and democracy: the battle for control of U.S. broadcasting 1927–1935*, Oxford University

Press, 1993.

Machlup, F., *The production and distribution of knowledge in the United States*, Princeton University Press, 1962.

Mandelson, P. and Liddle, R., *The Blair revolution: can New Labour deliver?*, Faber and Faber, 1996.

Marshall, A., Dot coma, *Independent*, 25 April 2001, Business Review, 1–2.

Martin, W. J., *The global information society*, 2nd edn, Aslib/Gower, 1995.

Marvin, C., *When old technologies were new: thinking about electric communication in the late nineteenth century*, Oxford University Press, 1988.

Masuda, Y., *The information society as post-industrial society*, Institute for the Information Society, 1980.

Masuda, Y., *Managing in the information society: releasing synergy Japanese style*, Basil Blackwell, 1990.

Meadows, A. J. (ed.), *The origins of information science*, Taylor Graham/Institute of Information Scientists, 1987.

Milton, J., *Areopagitica*, 1644.

Montviloff, V., *National information policies: a handbook on the formulation, approval, implementation and operation of a national policy on information*, UNESCO, 1990 (PGI-90/WS/11).

Moore, N., Is the global information society working? A review of progress in the member states of the European Union, *Alexandria*, **11** (1), 1999, 39–50.

Mouse Site, The Demo
http://sloan.stanford.edu/MouseSite/1968Demo.html

Napster signs deal with Bertelsmann
http://www.guardian.co.uk/Archive/Article/0,4273,4084305,00.html

Naughton, J., *A brief history of the future: the origins of the internet*, Weidenfeld & Nicolson, 1999.

Neil, A., *Full disclosure*, Pan, 1997.

Nelson, T., *Literary machines*, Mindful Press, 1982.

Nelson, T., *Computer lib*, rev. edn, Tempus Books, 1987.

Nelson, T., Miracle device: Feed's document on Ted Nelson's literary machines, *Feed Magazine*, January 1998
http://www.feedmag.com/templates/old_article.php3?a_id=1210

Nine billion g-mails per month
  http://www.cellular.co.za/news_2000/news-11262000_nine_ billion_sms.htm
Nua internet surveys: *1996 review,*
  http://www.nua.ie/surveys/1996review.html
Olson, D. R., *The world on paper: the conceptual and cognitive implications of reading and writing,* Cambridge University Press, 1994.
Ong, W. J., *The presence of the word: some prolegomena for cultural and religious history,* Yale University Press, 1967.
Ong, W. J., *Orality and literacy: the technologizing of the word,* Routledge, 1982.
Oppenheim, C. and MacMorrow, N., Information policy. In Feather, J. and Sturges, P. (eds), *International encyclopaedia of information and library science,* Routledge, 1997.
Organisation for Economic Co-operation and Development, *Globalisation of industrial activities. Four case studies: auto parts, chemicals, construction and semi-conductors,* OECD, 1992.
Outhwaite, W., *Habermas: a critical introduction,* Polity Press, 1994.
Paine, C., Doctors: society's whipping boys, *RSA Journal,* 4/1, 2001, 25–7.
Pope, I., *Internet UK,* Prentice Hall, 1995.
Porat, M. U., *The information economy: definition and measurement,* United States Dept of Commerce, Office of Telecommunications, 1977.
Prodi, R., *2000–2005: shaping the new Europe,* speech to the European Parliament, Strasbourg, 15 February 2000.
Ricci, A., Measuring the information society: dynamics of European data on usage of information and communication technologies in Europe since 1995, *Telematics and Informatics,* **17** (1–2), 2000, 141–67.
Rose, M. A., *The post-modern and the post-industrial: a critical analysis,* Cambridge University Press, 1991.
Rough Guides Ltd, *The internet and the world wide web: the rough guide,* 3rd edn, Rough Guides, 1998.
Rough Guides Ltd, *The internet and the world wide web: the rough guide,* 5th edn, Rough Guides, 2000.
Royal Society Scientific Information Conference, *Report and papers submitted,* The Royal Society, 1948.

Sabaratnam, J. S., Planning the library of the future: the Singapore experience, *IFLA Journal*, **23** (3), 1997, 197–202.

Sarup, M., *An introductory guide to post-structuralism and postmodernism*, 2nd edn, Harvester/Wheatsheaf, 1993.

Schiller, H. I., *Information and the crisis economy*, Ablex, 1984.

Schiller, H. I. et al., *The ideology of international communications*, Institute for Media Analysis, 1992.

Schudra, M., *Watergate in American memory*, Basic Books, 1992.

Scourias, J., Overview of the Global System for Mobile Communications
http://www.shoshin.uwaterloo.ca/~jscouria/GSM/gsmreport. html

Sengupta, K., GCHQ releases the secret details of how Bletchley Park built the first computer, *Independent*, 30 September 2000, 13.

Shannon, C. E., A mathematical theory of communication, *Bell Systems Technical Journal*, **27**, 1948, 379–423, 623–58.

Shannon, C. E. and Weaver, W., *The mathematical theory of communication*, University of Illinois Press, 1949.

Shera, J. H., Of librarianship, documentation and information science, *UNESCO Bulletin for Libraries*, **22** (2), 1968, 58–65.

Singh, S., *The code book: the secret history of codes and codebreaking*, Fourth Estate, 2000.

Spiegel, P., Regulations out of step on the issue of the internet, *Financial Times*, 13–14 January 2001, 20.

Standage, T., *The Victorian internet: the remarkable story of the telegraph and the 19th century's online pioneers*, Weidenfeld and Nicolson, 1998.

Stein, H. H. and Harkison, J. M., *Muckraking: past, present and future*, University of Pennsylvania Press, 1974.

Stone, P., Hume, C. and Smith, P., *Project EARL (Electronic Access to Resources in Libraries): networking for public libraries' information and resource sharing services via the Internet. Final Report*, British Library (BLRDD Innovation Report, 42), 1997.

Stonier, T., Towards a new theory of information, *Journal of Information Science*, **42** (5), 1991, 257–63.

Susskind, R., The impact of technology [on the professions], *RSA Journal*, 4/1, 2001, 21–2.

Swinson, C., Quality assurance, *RSA Journal*, 4/1, 2001, 23–4.

Tawfik, M. (ed.), *World communication and information report 1999-2000*
http://www.unesco.org/webworld/wcir/en.html

Travis, A., *Bound and gagged: a secret history of obscenity in Britain*, Profile Books, 2000.

Turing, A., On computable numbers, with an application to the *Entscheidungsproblem*, *Proceedings of the London Mathematical Society*, **42**, 1936, 230–65.

UNESCO, *Observatory on the information society*
http://www.unesco.org/webworld/observatory/index.html

Usborne, D., Yahoo! to ban trade in racist material on website, *Independent*, 4 January 2001, 12.

Vickers, A., AOL Time Warner merger through
http://www.mediaguardian.co.uk/city/story/00,7497,411534,00. html

Vickery, B. C., Bradford's law of scattering, *Journal of Documentation*, **4** (3), 1948, 198–203.

Vickery, B., The Royal Society scientific information conference of 1948, *Journal of Documentation*, **54** (3), 1998, 281–3.

Vickery, B., A century of scientific and technical information, *Journal of Documentation*, **55** (5), 1999, 476–527.

Von Heilmcrone, H., The efforts of the European Union to harmonise copyright and impact on freedom of information, *Libri*, **50** (1), 2000, 32–9.

Walker, D., Statistics show immigration beneficial to the economy
http://www.guardian.co.uk/Archive/article/0,4273,4126367,00. html

Walsh, N. P., 'Mom, I blew up the music industry', *Observer*, 21 May 2000
http://www.guardian.co.uk/Archive/Article/0,4273,4020371,00. html

Webster, F., *Theories of an information society*, Routledge, 1995.

Wells, M., Back with a bong, *Guardian*, 25 September 2000, Media, 2–5.

Wersig, G., Information science: the study of post-modern knowledge use, *Information Processing and Management*, **29**, 1993, 229–39.

White, T. H., *Breach of faith: the fall of Richard Nixon*, Athenaeum Publishers, 1975.

Wiener, N., *Cybernetics, or control and communication in the animal and the machine*, 2nd edn, MIT Press, 1961.

Williams, R., Let the MacGames begin
**http://www.observer.co.uk/Guardian/sydney/story/
0,7369,366355,00.html**

Winston, B., *Media, technology and society: a history: from the telegraph to the internet*, Routledge, 1998.

Winterbotham, F. W., *The Ultra secret*, Weidenfeld and Nicolson, 1974.

Yapp, C., The knowledge society: the challenge of transition, *Business Information Review*, **17** (2), 2000, 59–65.

Young, H., *One of us: a biography of Margaret Thatcher*, Pan, 1989.

Websites

We list here the websites that are cited in the text or references, with a brief note on the nature of the site and its relevance; we have made no attempt to make this a comprehensive listing of sites in the various categories. References to specific documents will normally be found in the Bibliography or in the notes and references accompanying each chapter. We have listed the sites in alphabetical order of their principal subjects.

Alan Turing
http://www.turing.org.uk/turing
A site devoted to Alan Turing, including bibliographies and analyses.

British government
http://www.ukonline.gov.uk
The official site of the UK government, with extensive links. This has recently been developed as a replacement for the older site at **http://www.open.gov.uk**.

Censorship, freedom of the press and freedom of information
http://artsreformation.com
Useful material on censorship of the arts, especially cinema and video.

http://www.cfoi.org.uk
The official site of the Campaign for Freedom of Information, an influential lobby group in the UK.

http://www.indexoncensorship.org
The online version of the long-established journal, including much invaluable data and analysis from all over the world.

http://www.privacyinternational.org
A privately maintained site, which has regularly updated information on freedom of information issues around the world, especially in the USA.

http://www.terramedia.com
Includes important articles on censorship in the UK and elsewhere.

http://www.cyber-rights.org/
A well-established and authoritative site that considers law and policy in cyberspace.

Data Protection Agency
http://www.dataprotection.gov.uk
The official site of the agency responsible for the enforcement of data protection law in the UK.

Department of Trade and Industry
http://www/dti.gov.uk
The site of the UK department of state that has responsibility for intellectual property and data protection.

Douglas Englebart
http://www.bootstrap.org/dce-bio.htm
http://sloan.stanford.edu/MouseSite/1968Demo.html
These are, respectively, a biographical account of Englebart, and a site devoted to what is perhaps his most visible contribution to computing!

E-commerce
http://www.egg.com
http://lastminute.com
Two examples of dot.com enterprises.

Electronic publishing

http://elseviersciencedirect.com
The site of a major online publisher of scientific journals.

http://www.onlineoriginals.com
A site giving access to works of fiction that have been published online.

http://www.stephenking.com
The site of the science fiction author, including details of his electronic publishing ventures.

European Union

http://www.europa.eu.int
The official site of the European Union. It is a unique and inescapable source for information about developments in the EU, and has a substantial (although not comprehensive) archive of documents. Its search engine is reasonably effective, although it is often better to go initially to particular areas of the site (such as the new Information Society site at **http://europa.eu.int/information_society/**) and then to make a detailed search. The site also gives access to European legislation, the proceedings of the European Parliament, and other related organizations and activities.

http://europa.eu.int/ISPO/
The Information Society Project Office (ISPO) site was the main site detailing the EU IS strategy. In May 2001, the ISPO site was archived; the latest news on strategy and policy can be now found at the Europa site.

http://europa.eu.int/ISPO/esis/default.htm
The ESIS (European Survey of Information Society Projects and Actions) site includes statistics on a range of information society projects. It also contains a range of detailed reports on information society indicators in EU member states.

Internet usage statistics

http://www.cyberatlas.internet.com
One of several sites which give usage statistics and other data about

the internet. This is usually up to date and includes some interesting analyses.

http://www.gip.int
The official site of the Global Inventory Project, sponsored by the G8 nations to record information society developments.

http://www.nua.ie
Another site with data about internet usage, with qualitative as well as quantitative analyses.

http://www.worldpaper.com
Includes the site of the Information Society Index (ISI), for which see Chapter 5, p 104 and note 17.

Memex
http://www.dynamicdiagrams.com/design/memex/model.htm
A demonstration of how the Memex was designed to work.

Mobile telephony
http://www.cellular.co.za
A South African commercial site with comprehensive statistical data and news coverage of the mobile telephony sector.

http://www.shoshin.uwaterloo.ca/~jscouria/GSM/gsmreport. html
An authoritative account of GSM.

Newspapers and press agencies
http://www.dailynews.yahoo.com
http://www.guardian.co.uk
http://mediaguardian.co.uk
http://www.observer.co.uk
http://www.nytimes.com
All of these sites are well constructed and comparatively easy to use, and all are of newspapers that regularly carry news (and often whole sections) on the media and on internet developments.

NHS Direct
http://www.nhsdirect.nhs.uk

An online medical information and advisory service developed by the National Health Service in the UK.

The People's Network
http://www.lic.gov.uk
The official site of the Library and Information Commission, which includes documents about the origins of the People's Network, the UK public access network based on public libraries. LIC no longer exists; its functions have been inherited by Re:source (**http://www.resource.gov.uk**).

http://www.peoplesnetwork.gov.uk
The official site of the People's Network.

The Rand Corporation
http://www.rand.org
The official site of the US think tank, which includes some important early papers on networks, including Paul Baran's report referred to in Chapter 2 (p 30, and note 17).

Search engines and other guides to the internet
http://www.roughguides.com
The site includes the online version of the Rough Guide to the internet and the web, referred to in Chapter 3 (p 51 and notes 5 and 11).

http://www.searchenginewatch.com
An evaluative guide to internet search engines.

http://www.zdnet.com
Information about Yahoo!'s guide to the 'best sites' referred to in Chapter 3 (see p 55, note 21).

Stockholm Challenge
http://www.challenge.stockholm.se
The official site for the annual global competition for information society developments (see above, p 117).

UNESCO
http://www.unesco.org

The official site of UNESCO, containing a great deal of invaluable data about ICT usage and other matters relating to the information society.

http://www.unesco.org/webworld/observatory/
The site of UNESCO's Information Observatory, which also has links to most information society strategies and policies from around the world.

University for Industry
http://www.learndirect.co.uk
The official site of the UK's network for lifelong learning.

http://www.learning.org.uk
A description of the latest UfI schemes.

Virtual universities
http://online.phoenix.edu
A private virtual university in the USA.

http://www.mit.edu
Includes details of MIT's distance learning plans (see above, p 144), which will, in due course, carry the learning materials as well.

Index